FARMING ENCYCLOPEDIAS

THE TRACTOR AND EQUIPMENT ENCYCLOPEDIA

BY DONNA B. McKINNEY

Encyclopedias

An Imprint of Abdo Reference

abdobooks.com

TABLE OF CONTENTS

HISTORY OF FARM EQUIPMENT

On some farms today, oxen are still used to pull plows.

For about 12,000 years, humans have been planting crops and raising animals on farms. As people first learned to farm, they settled into communities and towns. Before that time, people gathered plants and hunted animals for food. The earliest farms were in the Fertile Crescent. This area is in western Asia and northern Africa. Humans improved their metalworking skills about 5,000 years ago, at the beginning of what is known as the Bronze Age. With these skills, they began improving basic farming tools. They made axes and simple plows pulled by oxen.

By the 1700s, changes were happening in farm technology. In Britain, the Industrial Revolution was beginning and would soon spread to other parts of the world. Society was shifting from mostly farming to an economy led by industry and manufacturing. British inventors began using newly discovered technologies to make machines that helped farms be more productive.

In 1701 British inventor Jethro Tull made the seed drill. A horse pulled this device. The seed drill allowed farmers to plant three rows of seeds at a time. Before this, farmers used a simple plow to break the soil and dropped seeds by hand as they plowed. Some farmers continued using traditional ways to plant their crops. But Tull's seed drill eventually replaced the earlier methods of planting.

A 1955 painting by Alfred Reginald Thomson shows Jethro Tull with his seed drill.

The earliest tractors had steel wheels.

By the early 1800s, inventors were making steam engines to power farm machines. In 1812 British inventor Richard Trevithick made the barn engine. This machine was used to drive a corn thresher, which separated the kernels from the husks. Other threshing machines and saws were invented during the 1800s. With these machines, farmers harvested crops and built barns with less effort. Farm work began to shift from being powered by humans and animals to being powered by machines.

In 1903 American inventors Charles Hart and Charles Parr built a new type of self-propelled engine. Their machine was powered by gasoline. They named it the tractor. It pulled farm machinery such as plows. In the early 1900s, more companies began making tractors. By the 1930s, more than one million tractors had been sold in the United States. Tractor prices dropped as more tractors were produced. Even farmers who were not wealthy could buy a tractor.

During the 1950s and 1960s, companies continued to improve tractors and equipment. They tried different kinds of engines and tires. Farm productivity increased with these developments.

FARMING TODAY

The tractor is still vital to farm life. Modern tractors can be self-steering and guided by Global Positioning System (GPS) technology. Equipment such as plows and combines are regularly improved to be even more efficient. Farmers also use a variety of other high-tech farm equipment. Drones in the air and sensors in the ground are two ways farmers are using new technology to monitor their crops. Putting technology to work, today's farmers can manage crops and be more productive than ever.

Tablets are easily portable, allowing farmers to track information while they work on their large properties.

TRACTORS

WHAT IS A TRACTOR?

A tractor is a vehicle with a motor. It has large rear wheels and smaller front wheels. Or it has tracks. Tractors are used mainly on farms and are designed for off-road work. They are built for power, not speed, so they move slowly. They pull farm equipment and trailers. The word *tractor* comes from the Latin word *trahere*, meaning "to pull."

In 2021 more than 351,000 farm tractors were sold in the United States and Canada.

Farmers use tractors to pull equipment such as plows. Plows break up the soil deep down and mix the layers to remove weeds. Farmers also use tractors to cultivate the soil, loosening the top layer and preparing it for planting. Tractors help farmers plant seeds and harvest crops. Additional jobs for tractors include clearing land, spreading fertilizer, and mowing grass.

Steam engines powered the earliest tractors. Today internal combustion engines power tractors. These engines get energy by burning fuel inside their frames.

Farmers were using steam engine tractors in the 1870s.

Tracklaying tractors are also called crawlers or caterpillars.

Tracklaying tractors move like military tanks. Tracks give better traction than wheels in wet, muddy soil. Tracklaying tractors tend to be a little more expensive than wheel tractors.

General purpose tractors with four wheels or tracks come in different sizes. Although there can be differences in sizes between tractor brands, tractors are usually labeled as utility, compact, or subcompact. Standard-size utility tractors handle jobs in large fields. These tractors have 60 to 140 horsepower engines. Horsepower is the measurement of the power an engine produces. Most utility tractors are about 4.5 to 6 feet (1.4 to 1.8 m) wide.

Compact tractors have 25 to 60 horsepower engines. These tractors are about 3.5 to 4.5 feet (1.1 to 1.4 m) wide. Subcompact tractors have engines that are under 25 horsepower. They are usually less than 4 feet (1.2 m) wide. Both of these smaller tractors are used for landscaping or working in tight spaces, such as vineyards or orchards.

Standard-size utility tractors are strong enough to pull the heavy pieces of equipment needed to farm large areas of land efficiently.

Even smaller tractors are also available. Garden tractors are popular with some homeowners. These tractors are similar to riding lawn mowers but are a little sturdier. Lawn mowers have the engine in the middle or rear, while the engine is in the front in garden tractors. People use garden tractors to cut grass and tend small family gardens. These small tractors are also able to pull small equipment such as harrows. Harrows are tools that break up and level the soil.

Garden tractors are also called mini tractors.

The two-wheel tractor is also called the walk-behind, single-axle, or walking tractor.

An even smaller tractor is the two-wheel tractor. Two-wheel tractors are slower than other tractors because they are built to move at the speed of a person walking behind them. Two-wheel tractors can either pull or push farm equipment. These tractors can be useful for smaller farms of 20 acres (8 ha) or less. They are also less expensive than four-wheel tractors.

After World War II (1939–1945), many American farmers wanted bigger farms. They needed larger and more powerful tractors. But in more recent years, many people enjoy buying and eating locally grown food. Small-scale farms meet that need. Two-wheel tractors are gaining popularity with these small-scale farmers.

Farmers markets are a common place to purchase a variety of foods directly from farmers.

Steam engines burn fuel to heat water. The steam pushes against a piston, which generates motion that powers the tractor.

HISTORY OF TRACTORS

In the late 1800s, farmers began using steam engines to haul plows. In 1890 John Froelich of Iowa built the first farm vehicle powered by a gasoline-fueled internal combustion engine. Froelich's machine could carry a much larger load of grain than any other vehicle at that time.

The early traction engines, which were tractors powered by steam, were later called steam tractors. But they were very heavy, weighing more than 15 tons (13.6 metric tons), and complex to operate. And there was the danger of the steam engines exploding. These early machines never became popular.

Other automobile plows were in use around the world, including in the United Kingdom, at the time Ford built his.

Hart and Parr built the first US factory for making gas traction engines in about 1900. Then they built their self-propelled traction machine in the early 1900s. This machine made them the first people to successfully sell tractors commercially in the United States. In 1907 Henry Ford built his first gas-powered tractor. This machine was called an automobile plow.

Those earliest gas-powered tractors were similar to steam engine tractors. They were very large, weighing 10 to 15 tons

(9.1 to 13.6 metric tons). They moved on big steel wheels or tracks. But tractor companies were soon working to build smaller, less expensive tractors. These smaller tractors weighed about 1 to 3 tons (0.9 to 2.7 metric tons). Ford built the first successful small tractor, called the Fordson, in 1917. It was the first general-purpose tractor to be lightweight, small, and easy to maneuver. The average farmer could afford to purchase a Fordson. It soon became the most popular tractor in the United States.

Ford had sold more than 35,000 Fordson tractors by 1921.

Farmers used large, muscular draft horses to pull plows. The Clydesdale is one draft horse breed.

Before tractors, farmers used horses and mules to pull equipment like plows and mowers. As tractors became more popular, farmers rebuilt these tools to be pulled by tractors. But the early tractors were heavy, had large steel wheels, and rode close to the ground. They would damage tall crops like corn or cotton.

In the tractor's early days, equipment the tractor pulled was powered only by its turning wheels. For example, the rotation of the wheels was turned into the spinning motion of a mower's blades. In 1922 International Harvester Company (IH) invented the power take-off (PTO). This device allowed the tractor engine to power both the tractor and the equipment it pulled, giving the equipment more power than it could get just by turning wheels. Soon tractor companies were redesigning tractor equipment to be used with the PTO.

The spinning motion of the power take-off, *black and gold bar*, powers the equipment.

In the 1920s, many tractors were made on assembly lines. People would do the same work, such as apply paint, on each tractor that passed by.

IH built a general-purpose tractor called the Farmall in 1923. This lightweight tractor had especially small front wheels. The Farmall could plow and cut like the Fordson. But unlike the Fordson, the Farmall could also work while crops were growing. The bottom of the tractor was high enough to drive through a field without damaging the crops. Soon other tractor companies such as Massey-Harris, Deere & Company, and Case were building their own general-purpose tractors.

In the late 1920s, Irish engineer Harry Ferguson invented the three-point hitch. It was called the Ferguson System. This device, still in use, is fastened to the rear of the tractor. It provides three points of connection between the tractor and the equipment. The hitch helps keep the equipment stable on uneven ground. Starting in 1937, Ford worked with Ferguson to develop tractors with the three-point hitch. Other companies began adding this hitch to their tractors too.

In 1939 Harry Ferguson, *left*, showed Henry Ford a tractor he invented.

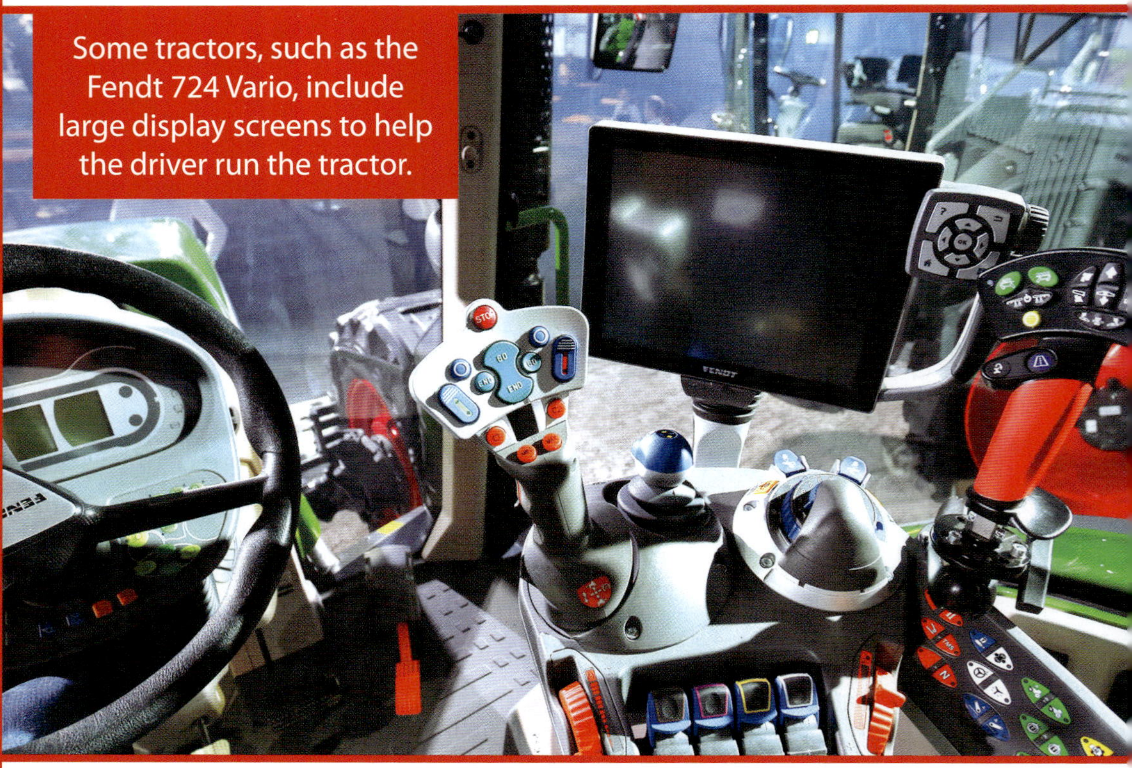

Some tractors, such as the Fendt 724 Vario, include large display screens to help the driver run the tractor.

By the late 1930s, most tractor companies were building the basic types of tractors farmers use today. But modern tractors are more comfortable than the early tractors. The cabs can now be enclosed and have heat, air-conditioning, stereos, and computer equipment. Some modern tractors are still powered by gasoline. But there are also tractor engines made for kerosene, liquefied petroleum gas, or diesel fuel.

HOW TRACTORS CHANGED FARMING

With the invention of the tractor, farmers' lives were forever changed. Farming still requires

hard work. But with the tractor, farmers could work much faster and more efficiently.

By the 1910s, more than 150 companies were making and selling tractors to American farmers. These companies drastically cut the prices of their tractors to compete with each other. With the low tractor prices, thousands of small farm owners were able to buy one. In 1916 American farmers bought more than 20,000 tractors. That number rose to one million tractors by 1935.

Many tractors in the early and mid-1900s were not especially large. It was more important to farmers that the tractors were affordable.

In the early 1900s, some farmers used both tractors and draft animals to pull equipment.

As more farmers bought tractors, many farm jobs became machine powered. Inventors saw the potential for what the tractor could do. They created a range of equipment that attached to the tractor to perform different tasks. Farmers used tractors to plow soil and plant seeds. Equipment attached to tractors helped fertilize and harvest crops. Tractors could also move supplies and equipment.

Working with a tractor, farmers could plant seeds quickly at the right time. They could get many seeds in the ground before the weather changed. They could also more quickly harvest crops at their peak.

The arrival of tractors decreased the farmer's need for horses and mules. In the 1920s, Americans owned more than 25 million horses and mules. Most of these animals worked on farms. By 1945 the number of horses and mules had shrunk to 2.5 million. The 1950 US census reported a direct connection between the drop in the number of these animals and the increase in tractors. Owning a tractor reduced costs because farmers did not need the food and land required to care for horses and mules.

When farmers relied on draft animals, they needed to set aside some of their land for the animals to graze. Horses eat approximately 1.5 to 2 percent of their weight in dry food each day.

Soybeans are used to make tofu, soy milk, and many other products.

When farmers no longer needed as many animals to work the land, they could raise other crops that brought in more money. Many farmers began raising soybeans. This crop has become the second most valuable US crop after corn. It is used as animal feed and in vegetable oil and other food products.

The tractor also changed the lives of people who worked on farms. Children in farm families often helped with farm work starting at a young age. With the tractor, not as many farm workers were needed. Children were able to spend less time helping on the farm and more time in school. Fewer adults were needed for farm work too. Some adults moved from farms to cities to work in manufacturing jobs.

HOW DO TRACTORS WORK?

Some vehicles with powerful engines, such as race cars, use their engines to move fast. But tractors need powerful engines to pull heavy equipment and loads. They may need to pull thousands of pounds of weight.

Although children who live on American farms do not need to work like they did in the past, many still help their families run the farm.

Tractors can pull trailers loaded with livestock.

Tractors' engines are in the front. Small tractors might have gasoline engines. Large tractors have diesel engines. Diesel engines can provide strong pulling power at low speeds.

Tractors have two ways to pull equipment. These are the drawbar and the three-point hitch. They are located at the rear of the tractor.

The drawbar is a steel bar on the back of the tractor. The farmer attaches equipment to the drawbar at a single connection point so the tractor can pull the equipment. The drawbar cannot lift equipment off the ground.

The three-point hitch is another way to attach equipment to the tractor. Like the drawbar, it pulls equipment. But unlike the drawbar, it can lift equipment. A farmer might need to move a cultivator from one field to another without disturbing the ground. The hitch can lift the equipment off the ground to do this.

The PTO, *black bar*, and three-point hitch, *green and gray bars*, have been key parts of tractors for many decades.

A tractor must be able to lift some equipment, such as subsoilers, off the ground so they don't dig into ground the farmer does not want disturbed.

The hitch has hydraulic arms that lower and raise the equipment. With hydraulics, a pump pushes oil through hoses. This high-pressure oil pushes against a piston, forcing it to move. The movement of this piston lifts the equipment. The hitch also helps the tractor pull equipment across uneven ground. Because the equipment is attached to the tractor at three different points, the equipment remains more stable.

In addition to helping tractors pull, the engine can help run equipment attached to the tractor. A PTO shaft makes a connection between equipment and the tractor. This shaft cannot pull the equipment, so it is used along with a drawbar or three-point hitch. The tractor's engine rotates the shaft. This rotation transfers power to the equipment attached to the tractor. For example, it might power a conveyor belt on a combine. Some tractors also have a PTO in the front. This allows the farmer to use equipment at the front and back at the same time.

A tractor might have a hay spear attached to its front to help it move hay bales.

Tractor tires can be designed to fit between rows of crops.

Tractors often have large tires. The back tires are bigger than the front tires. The tires are wide to help spread out the tractor's weight on the field so the tractor packs down the soil as little as possible. Wide tires also help keep the tractor from sinking into mud and becoming stuck. Deep treads help the tires grip rough ground.

HOW ARE TRACTORS USED?

Farmers grow many types of crops. They can choose from a variety of tractors based on the job. Standard-size wheel tractors can be used for many purposes, such as to pull or push a wide range of equipment. Depending on the equipment attached to the tractor, farmers can plow the soil or pull weeds. They can plant seeds or harvest crops.

Compact tractors are typically used in small fields and for yard work. They gained popularity in Japan in the 1970s. Farms there are usually smaller than in the United States. The amount of land that can be worked with equipment is limited. Japanese farmers needed tractors that were small and easy to maneuver. Once tractor companies began making compact tractors, their popularity spread beyond Japan.

People can use compact tractors for their personal gardens.

Farmers use tracklaying tractors in sticky soil or light soil that is difficult for tires to grip. These tractors are also useful on hillsides or rough fields. Orchard farmers might use orchard tractors. These tractors are slim to fit between rows of trees. Tractor attachments that shake the nuts or fruit out of trees are available.

Tractors don't only help with crop farming. They also help with livestock care. Farmers use tractors to move large amounts of feed to barns and pastures.

Tractors can help clear land. They move piles of dirt, rocks, brush, or dead trees using a hinged bucket called a front-end loader. The tractor can cut heavy grasses or brush with a mower. Farmers might also attach a brush puller that pulls up small trees.

Orchard tractors are also called fruit tractors.

A front-end loader can help farmers move animal feed.

Tractors fitted with snowblowers can move the snow they collect into a truck to be dumped elsewhere.

In areas that get winter snowstorms, the tractor can be useful for snow removal. Farmers can attach a front-end loader to push and clear snow from roads and other areas. A tractor can also pull out a car that has slid into a ditch.

Tractors can do all kinds of work. They can also provide fun. A tractor can pull a wagon filled with bales of hay so people can enjoy hayrides.

TOMORROW'S TRACTORS

Tractors have gone through huge changes since they were invented more than 100 years ago. The tractor continues to play a key role in farm life. This machine keeps changing as

advances in technology bring more improvements. Decades ago, farmers wanted bigger, more powerful tractors. Today, one focus is on building tractors that are environmentally friendly. Robotics and artificial intelligence will play an important role in the tractors of the future. Artificial intelligence uses computer systems to imitate the ways humans make decisions and solve problems.

John Deere displayed the 8R, a self-driving tractor, at the 2022 CES (formerly Consumer Electronics Show).

John Deere developed StarFire, a GPS guidance system. Its uses include guiding a tractor so it can precisely drive between rows of crops.

Tractors can use GPS technology. GPS helps farmers map their fields, sample the soil, and observe how crops are doing. Using a tractor with GPS, farmers can mark specific locations in their fields for collecting soil samples. They return to those spots year after year to gather soil samples and monitor the health of the crops. And with GPS guiding the way, farmers can work when the visibility is low, such as during dust storms, fog, or rain. Tractor companies continue to refine GPS technology and find new ways to put it to work.

Tractor companies are already building and testing autonomous tractors. These machines use advanced cameras and computers to map the land where the tractor is moving. They use many of the same sensors found in self-driving cars.

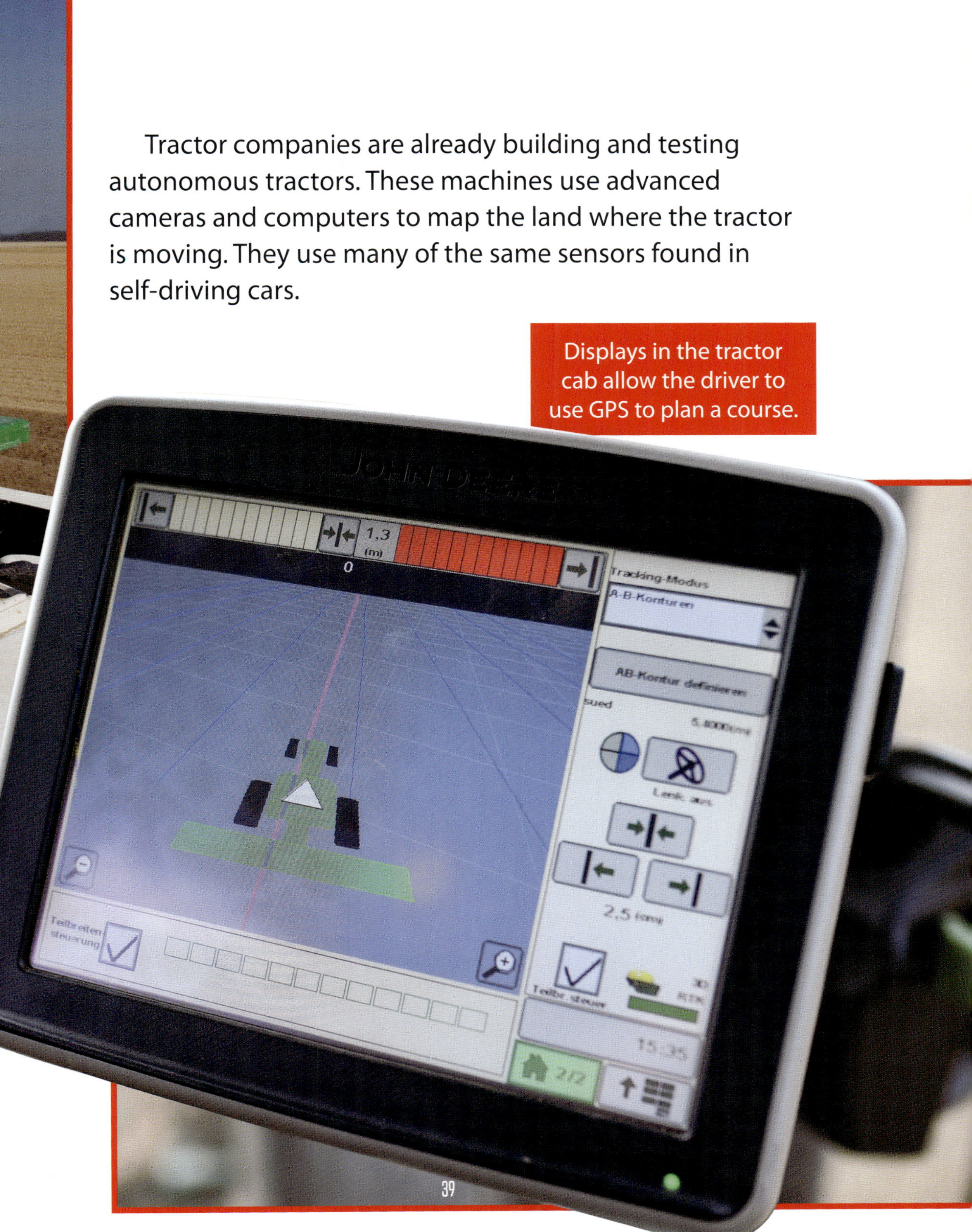

Displays in the tractor cab allow the driver to use GPS to plan a course.

Companies have been developing self-driving tractors for several years. Robot Makers GmbH demonstrated a self-driving tractor in 2019 in Germany.

Artificial intelligence studies camera images and sensor information. It then makes quick decisions about where the tractor needs to drive. A computer can steer the tractor on its path. The farmer can still choose to drive these tractors by hand or control them with a computer device, such as a tablet. Some large tractors could be replaced by self-propelled autonomous machines, such as sprayers for orchards and vineyards. The sprayers apply liquid fertilizers, herbicides, or pesticides. These chemicals supply nutrients to crops or fight weeds and pests that might attack the crops.

Researchers are developing small robotic tractors that can work in groups. Using artificial intelligence, these small tractors could work together like an insect swarm to complete a farming task. Because these robotic tractors are lightweight, they could work in fields where heavier tractors cannot be used.

Swarm technology has already been used with drones. This technology could be modified for tractors.

In 2021 H2Trac sold its first EOX-175 electric tractor. The tractor's wheel spacing could be adjusted for different row widths, and it could angle all of its wheels in a circle to pivot the cab from a central point.

Tractor companies are also working to make future tractors more energy efficient. They are building tractors powered by electric motors. These electric tractors do not pollute the environment the way tractors powered by fossil fuels such as gasoline do. Electric tractors also require less maintenance than gasoline-powered tractors, so they save the farmer money in repair costs. Researchers are also looking at ways to use more biofuels in tractor engines. Biofuels are made from plants or from animal waste. These fuels release less air pollution than fossil fuels when burned.

Farmers are using computers to help them better manage their farms and have more productive crops. This application of technology is called precision agriculture or satellite agriculture. The farmer uses software and special sensors to get data about the condition of the soil, crops, and weather. The sensors gather data about the moisture in the soil and temperature of the air and soil. Satellites and drones provide the farmer with images of crops.

Agronomists are scientists who study soil and crops. They work with farmers, using technology to gather data about the soil so they can help crops grow well.

Farmers can use a technique called multiple cropping to encourage healthy soil. Also called polyculture, it involves planting multiple crops in a field during one growing season.

Using the data collected by satellites and drones, software helps the farmer make decisions about when to plant and harvest crops, how to manage the soil, and how to rotate crops. Crop rotation involves planting a series of different crops on the same land. For example, farmers may plant corn one year, soybeans the next year, and wheat the third year. This practice helps the soil stay healthier.

Tractors are an important part of precision agriculture. Computer software can guide the farmer in where and how to use the tractors. Precision agriculture also helps farmers schedule tractor maintenance. This keeps tractors in good condition so the farm runs efficiently.

Regular maintenance helps reduce the risk of more costly tractor repairs.

TRACTOR MANUFACTURERS

Edward P. Allis was one of the founders of Allis-Chalmers.

ALLIS-CHALMERS

Many manufacturers have played an important role in producing tractors. The Allis-Chalmers company started in 1847 in Wisconsin. It made iron products. For decades it grew in size and in the scope of products it produced. It was a leading company making engines and machines. In the 1910s, Allis-Chalmers started making tractors. By the 1930s, it was one of the leading farm machinery companies in the United States.

Allis-Chalmers continued to grow. During World War I (1914–1918) and World War II, it produced parts for weapons, ships, and planes. But in the 1980s, Allis-Chalmers struggled. It fell behind other companies producing the same kinds of products. In 1999, the company closed.

TRACTOR MODELS

Allis-Chalmers tractors were orange. The company produced the Model U from 1929 to 1952. The Model U tractor was the first farm tractor with rubber tires. Before this, tractors had steel wheels. With rubber tires, the tractors used less fuel. This is because the rubber tires have less resistance when rolling than steel wheels do. By 1940 most tractors were made with rubber tires.

The Allis-Chalmers Model U tractors were built in Wisconsin.

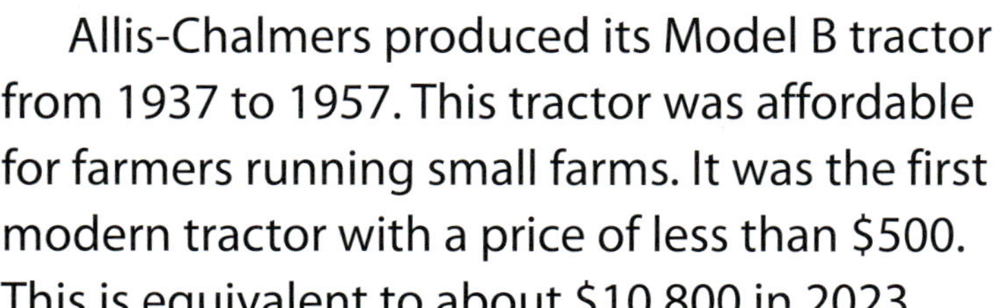

Allis-Chalmers produced its Model B tractor from 1937 to 1957. This tractor was affordable for farmers running small farms. It was the first modern tractor with a price of less than $500. This is equivalent to about $10,800 in 2023 dollars. With the arrival of the affordable Model B, many farmers who had been using horses to farm were able to buy their first tractors.

In 1948 Allis-Chalmers introduced the Model G tractor. The engine was mounted in the back instead of in the front. With the engine behind them, farmers could easily see where they were plowing or planting. This clear view of the field was especially useful for farmers working with small vegetables or berries that grew close to the ground.

More than 100,000 Allis-Chalmers Model B tractors were built.

The Allis-Chalmers D19 was sold from 1961 to 1964.

ADDING MORE POWER

By the 1960s, tractor companies pushed to offer engines with more horsepower. Allis-Chalmers introduced the D19 tractor in 1961. The 58 horsepower model was the first to add a turbocharger to the diesel engine. This device forces more air into the engine, providing additional oxygen so more fuel can burn at one time. This increases the engine's power.

By the late 1960s, Allis-Chalmers and other tractor companies began to focus on tractors that could pull equipment more quickly. Allis-Chalmers introduced the 220 Landhandler tractor in 1969. This tractor could pull heavy farm equipment faster than previous Allis-Chalmers models.

In addition to selling tractors, Case IH provides financial services to farmers.

CASE IH

Case IH started out as two separate companies. Case and International Harvester were two companies with a long history of building farming machines. In 1985 the two companies joined to form Case IH.

Jerome Case started Racine Threshing Machine Works in 1842. He built threshers, which farmers used to separate the grain from the plant stalks and husks. The company's name later changed to J. I. Case and Company. Cyrus McCormick started the McCormick Harvesting Machine Company in 1847. The name later became International Harvester (IH).

By 1869 Case's company was building the first steam engine tractor. Horses pulled this tractor. But it used a steam engine to power other farm equipment, such as saws or threshing machines. When the Great Chicago Fire destroyed McCormick's factory in 1871, Case offered to produce machines for McCormick.

Jerome Increase Case was 21 years old when he founded his business.

McCormick bought some other small companies to form International Harvester in 1902. IH produced the large and powerful Titan tractor in 1910. For several years, the Titan was a popular

The International Harvester Company was created in 1902 when five smaller companies merged.

tractor with American farmers. By 1917 IH was the biggest American tractor company.

THE FARMALL AND MORE

In 1923 IH built the Farmall tractor. The company wanted a tractor that could compete with the popular Fordson tractor made by Ford. The lightweight Farmall tractor remained popular with farmers for decades.

IH's Titan tractor sold until 1920.

The Farmall looked something like a tricycle. It had two small wheels in the front. They were positioned close together. The large rear wheels had heavy treads. The design made it practical for farming crops in rows. The Farmall also had a PTO to run the equipment the tractor pulled.

At first, IH built 200 Farmall tractors. Because of the model's popularity, within several years the company had built 9,500 Farmalls. It then made some updates to the Farmall. By 1932 it had produced 131,000 of the tractors. The Farmall's popularity grew quickly because it was so easy to use and could do a variety of farm tasks well.

This tractor had an important influence on the way farmers worked. When farmers plowed with animals, they usually planted their crops in grid patterns on small fields. This was an efficient way to plant crops when working with tools powered by hand and animals. But it was difficult to work in grids with tractors. Farmers then began planting crops in rows. Farmers could also work more land using a tractor, so their fields became bigger.

The original Farmall model later became known as the Farmall Regular.

IH also built the Farmall Culti-Vision. On this tractor, the farmer's seat was positioned to one side instead of directly in the center. The seat position gave the farmer a better view of crop rows while driving the tractor.

Meanwhile, Case produced its first diesel-engine tractor in 1953. It was the model 500. The company also made B series tractors in 1958. Farmers could choose from many options to best meet the needs of row-crop, rice, or orchard farming.

In the mid-1950s and early 1960s, IH released its number series Farmall tractors. The Farmall 1206 tractor was the first row-crop tractor to have an engine with more than 100 horsepower. Row-crop tractors sit high off the ground with the tires positioned to move between rows without damaging crops. In 1974 the company produced its five millionth tractor, a Farmall 1066 Turbo.

In 1984 Case built the Model 4994 tractor. It was the most powerful tractor the company had produced. It had a turbocharged engine.

Starting in 1955, Case sold a 400 series tractor with a diesel engine. It sold more than 2,000 of these tractors over two years.

JOINING FORCES

In the late 1980s, Case and International Harvester merged into one company called Case IH. This new company was the second-largest farm equipment company at that time. The Magnum tractor, built in 1987, was the first tractor Case IH produced.

Today Case IH produces standard-size tractors as well as compact and specialty tractors. They come in four-wheel and track models. The models Case IH produces include the Steiger series, Magnum series, Optum series, Puma series, Maxxum series, and Vestrum series. In 2003 the company reintroduced the Farmall tractor. This modern Farmall is compact and designed for small farms.

Case IH sells 10 versions of its Magnum tractor.

August Claas's son, Helmut, served on the CLAAS board from 1978 until 2010, when his daughter took his place.

CLAAS

CLAAS is a German company started in 1913 by brothers August, Franz, Theo, and Bernhard Claas. They originally called the company Claas Brothers. The company made a harvesting machine called a straw binder. The straw binder cuts the plants, bundles them together, and ties them with string.

When World War I started, the brothers were called to serve in the German military. When they returned from the war, the brothers purchased an old building and some land. They turned it into a straw binder factory. But right after the war, materials were hard to find. Gathering up any old straw binders they could find, they repaired and improved the old binders and resold them. Soon they had the money and supplies they needed to restart their business.

COMBINES AND TRACTORS

During the 1930s, CLAAS turned its attention to making combines. A combine cuts grain and then separates the grain from the chaff. Chaff includes seed coverings and other discarded plant parts.

The company saw how these machines were being used on American farms to quickly harvest large amounts of crops. European grain had much longer stalks and more moisture than American grain. The combines used in the United States would not work because the European grain wrapped around the combine's drums and got stuck. So CLAAS built a combine specifically for farming in Europe.

Combines separate the grain, *right*, from the chaff, *left*.

The CLAAS Axion tractor was first sold in 2006.

It began selling this combine in 1936. This machine cut the grain, threshed it, and bound it all in one step. It let European farmers harvest grain more quickly.

By 1968 CLAAS had produced 200,000 combines. The company became one of the leading combine companies in the world. It continued to grow, adding mowers and balers to its products. A baler is a machine that cuts crops such as hay, cotton, or straw and forms them into square or round bales. The bales can be easily moved off the field and stored.

For years CLAAS had pursued plans to design a tractor. In 2008 CLAAS bought the Renault Agriculture company. Renault was already making tractors, so CLAAS then had all it needed

to make its plans reality. Today CLAAS sells tractor models including the Arion, Axion, and Xerion. The Arion does many jobs on farms and ranches. It has up to 205 horsepower. The Axion is fuel efficient. The Xerion has up to 530 horsepower and is used on large commercial farms.

In 2023 a new Xerion tractor cost more than $600,000.

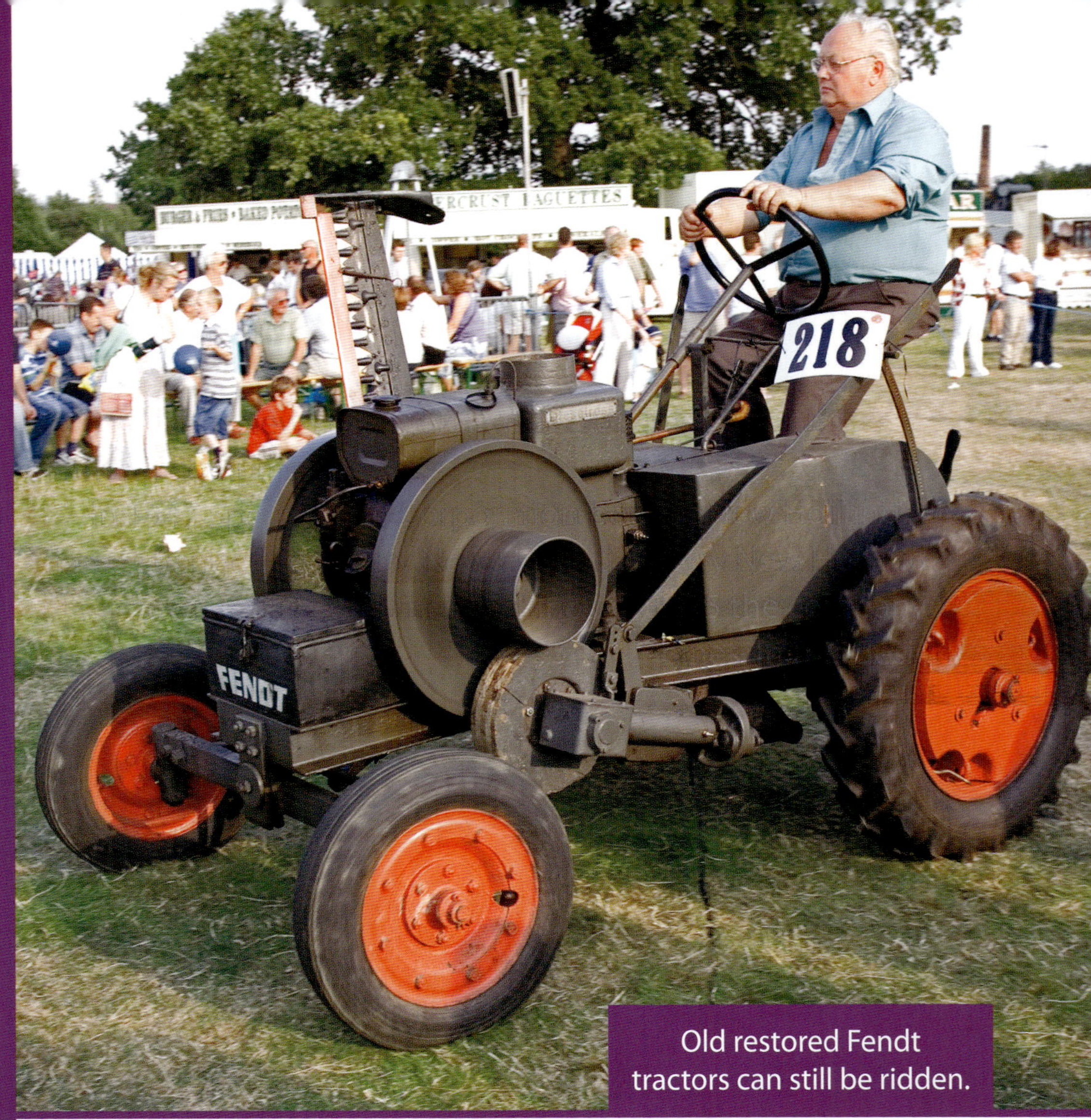

Old restored Fendt tractors can still be ridden.

FENDT

Fendt started as a clock-making business in Germany in 1635. Over time, it also made metal products. By the 1920s, it added farm machinery.

Around 1930, Fendt produced its first tractor, called the Dieselross. In German, the name means "diesel horse." This small 6 horsepower tractor could pull a mower and a plow.

When World War II started, Fendt was the second-largest German tractor company. But during the war years, Fendt focused on producing items for the military. The war had another impact on Fendt. Because of fuel shortages, farmers did not have access to gasoline. So companies built tractors that could be fueled by burning either wood or gasoline.

However, using wood as fuel caused some problems. Fresh wood had to be loaded in the tractor every couple of hours. There was also a delay while the farmer waited for the generator to get hot. During the war years, Fendt built about 1,400 wood-fueled tractors.

Brothers Xaver and Hermann Fendt invented the Dieselross.

STEPPING UP PRODUCTION

After World War II ended, Fendt's tractor production increased. The Fendt F12GT tractor had a large space for carrying items at the front of the tractor. This tractor was widely used among farmers in Germany and other European countries.

Fendt invests a lot of money into research and development. The company introduced cutting-edge tractor technology, such as suspended cabs in the 1970s. A suspended tractor cab rests on a system of shock absorbers. This feature gives the farmer a smoother, less bumpy ride over rough terrain.

In 2023, Fendt sold nine tractor varieties.

A US company named AGCO took note of Fendt's advanced design ideas and bought the company in 1997. It continues to build tractors, combines, and baling equipment under the Fendt name.

FORD

The Ford Motor Company was a pioneer in making cars widely available. It was also a leader in building tractors for American farmers. Ford built an experimental tractor in 1907. Owner Henry Ford called it an automobile plow.

Henry Ford founded the Ford Motor Company in 1903.

In 1917 Ford built its first tractor for sale to farmers, the Fordson. Just like Ford's cars, the Fordson tractor was built on an assembly line. This process made the tractor much cheaper than others at the time. Before the Fordson, tractors sold for $1,000 to $3,000 ($28,000 to $85,000 in 2023 dollars). That price range made it an impossible purchase for many farmers. But in 1918, the Fordson sold for $785 ($15,700 in 2023 dollars).

Ford popularized the assembly line. Its success in vehicle manufacturing encouraged other companies to use the method.

The Fordson was small, lightweight, and reliable, making it instantly popular.

The Fordson was a huge success. In just a decade, almost 850,000 had been built. The Fordson dominated the tractor market in the 1920s. It was no more advanced than other tractors at that time. But it did have unit frame construction instead of a traditional tractor frame. This meant that the engine block, the transmission, and the rear axle were all made together in one piece. With the success of the Fordson, all tractors soon used unit frame construction.

When the US economy took a downturn after World War I, Ford dropped the price to $395 ($7,900 in 2023 dollars). His strategy worked. Farmers bought Fordsons in record numbers. Ford stopped producing Fordson tractors for the US market in 1928. However, Fordson tractors would continue being built in England until 1964.

Henry Ford, *left*, grew up on a farm.

The Ford-Ferguson 9N was first built in Michigan.

MORE MODELS

From 1939 to 1946, Ford built the Ford-Ferguson 9N. This was the first US-made tractor to have a three-point hitch for connecting equipment to the tractor. In creating the 9N, Ford used some existing parts from Ford car engines in the tractor. This allowed Ford to keep the 9N's price affordable.

In 1955 Ford introduced its Hundred series tractors. Ford built these tractors in two power classes, the 600 and 800. Some of the Hundred series tractors were general utility tractors. Others had a higher ground clearance for row-crop work. The row-crop tractors could handle front-mounted equipment.

Starting in 1957, Ford introduced the 1 series tractors. All of these model numbers ended in the number one, such as 601 and 701. The 601 tractors were general utility tractors. The 701 tractors were row-crop tractors. Buyers could select tractors with or without options such as a PTO or three-point hitch.

In 1961 Ford introduced its Thousand series tractors. These tractors had more power than Ford's earlier tractors. The Ford 6000, the most powerful of the Thousand series, had a 60 horsepower diesel engine. With the Thousand series, Ford changed its tractor color scheme from red and white to blue and white.

Ford tractors changed a lot over time. A Ford tractor from the 1940s, *left*, had rubber tires and a different shape than earlier models.

The first Ford 4000s were sold in 1965.

In 1965 Ford streamlined its tractor business. Before this time, Ford had built separate tractors for the US and European markets. Now it kept just the Thousand series numbering, which is sold in both the United States and Europe. But it increased the horsepower for most of the tractor models.

In 1986 Ford bought the Sperry New Holland farm equipment company and named the new company Ford New Holland. Then in 1991, Ford sold its tractor business to the Italian company Fiat. Fiat used the Ford New Holland name until 1999. Then it dropped the Ford name from its tractors.

JOHN DEERE

John Deere was a blacksmith working in Vermont in the 1830s. The US economy began to struggle around 1837. So Deere and his family headed west to find new work opportunities. They settled in Illinois. Deere knew how to make farm tools that worked well in the sandy soil of Vermont. But the prairie soil in Illinois was different. Farmers constantly had to stop

John Deere was born in Rutland, Vermont, in 1804.

while plowing to scrape the sticky soil off the rough iron plow blades. So Deere thought up a solution.

Deere decided that shaping the plow blade a different way would help. He created a curved plow blade and made his plow out of steel, not iron. He figured less dirt would stick to the steel. Deere's steel plow was a success. By 1849, he was making 2,000 plows each year. Deere's blacksmith shop took on the name Deere & Company in 1868. It became commonly known as John Deere.

John Deere's improvements to the plow launched a successful career.

In the early 1900s, the company was very successful in selling plows and other farm equipment. It did not yet sell tractors. But tractors and plows were typically sold together. So John Deere felt pressure to sell tractors too.

MAKING TRACTORS

By 1917 the company had invented a three-wheel tractor called the All-Wheel-Drive tractor. This tractor was fuel efficient, it had great traction, and the engine was powerful. But at $1,200 ($31,400 in 2023 dollars), the tractor was expensive compared to other tractors at the time. Only 90 of the tractors sold.

After the disappointing sales for the All-Wheel-Drive, John Deere looked at other ideas. In 1918 it bought the Waterloo Gasoline Engine Company. That company already made a tractor called the Waterloo Boy. John Deere began selling it for about $700 ($15,300 in 2023 dollars). It improved the tractor by increasing the engine power while also making the tractor more compact. Yet the Waterloo Boy could not compete with Ford's Fordson tractor. So John Deere began working on new designs.

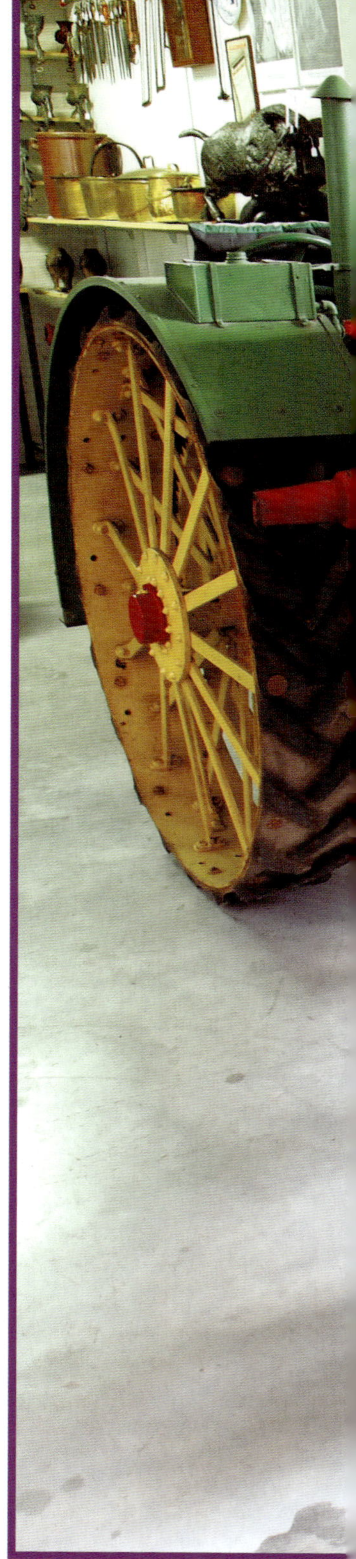

More than 21,000 Waterloo Boys were built.

During the 1940s, John Deere tractors were used on farms and were also used to pull army equipment in World War II.

In 1924 John Deere began selling the Model D tractor. It continued selling this popular tractor for almost 30 years. The company launched the Model A in 1934, followed by the Model B, a smaller version of the A.

In the 1950s, the company officially changed its name to John Deere. Starting in 1952, John Deere began selling its numbered series of tractors. These included the 40, 50, 60, 70, and 80. These tractors had more powerful engines and transmissions than earlier tractors. They also had power steering and a three-point hitch. In 1961 John Deere introduced the 1010, 2010, 3010, and 4010. These tractors had considerably more horsepower with barely any more weight than previous tractor models.

In the 1990s, John Deere introduced its 8000 series tractors. These tractors have a very tight turning radius that allows farmers to work in small spaces. In 2011 John Deere released its line of subcompact tractors, the 1023E and later the 1025R. These tractors are built for smaller jobs, such as mowing brush and weeds, removing snow, and tilling gardens. Tilling goes a bit deeper than cultivating, but not as deep as plowing.

John Deere tractors remain popular with farmers. It is one of the best-known tractor brands in the United States.

Kubota continues making iron pipes today.

KUBOTA

Kubota began as a metal workshop in Japan in 1890. It made iron pipes that delivered drinking water to homes. By 1922 Kubota was making oil engines for farming jobs. For decades, Kubota focused its work on engines.

After World War II, Kubota began making cultivators. By the 1950s, it expanded the farm machinery part of its business. It offered training for people wanting to learn to use its farm equipment. In 1960 it introduced its first rider-driven tractor, called the T15. By 1972 Kubota was selling its tractors in the United States. It opened a location in Compton, California. Kubota tractors were diesel powered. At that time, diesel engines in the United States had a reputation for being noisy and frequently breaking down. But Kubota built dependable diesel engines, and its tractors sold very well in the United States.

Today Kubota sells a wide range of farming equipment, including tractors, mowers, utility vehicles, and more.

Farmers can use mini excavators to move hay bales and till soil.

ADDING EQUIPMENT

In the late 1960s and early 1970s, Kubota focused on building farm equipment in addition to tractors. It began selling a three-row reaper-binder in 1965. This device harvests the crop and binds it with string. To meet the needs of small-scale farmers, Kubota introduced a two-row reaper-binder. The reaper-binders were popular with rice farmers. In 1971 Kubota began selling a combine with a front driving seat. This combine was popular with Japanese farmers. Kubota expanded the sale of its farm equipment three years later. It began selling in France, West Germany, the Netherlands, and Switzerland. That same year, Kubota decided to focus on building compact vehicles. Its mini excavator, used for digging or loading large items, was released in 1974 and became very popular.

In 1989 Kubota opened a US plant in Georgia. This plant made farm equipment. The company wanted to focus on products that were tailored to the local market. Having US plants helped the company market its equipment to American farmers.

SMALL TRACTORS

Kubota built the first subcompact tractor in 2000. It was called the BX series. Soon other tractor companies began making subcompacts. Subcompact tractors are typically the smallest tractors. They are built for use in gardens and on lawns. In 2002 Kubota made the BX23. This was the first subcompact tractor with a front loader and backhoe attached. In 2004 Kubota started building four-wheel-drive utility task vehicles (UTVs). These vehicles used the same technologies as Kubota's tractors, including the compact diesel engine.

Kubota's small tractors can pull personal boats and other small loads.

Kubota's compact tractors can be used in grape vineyards.

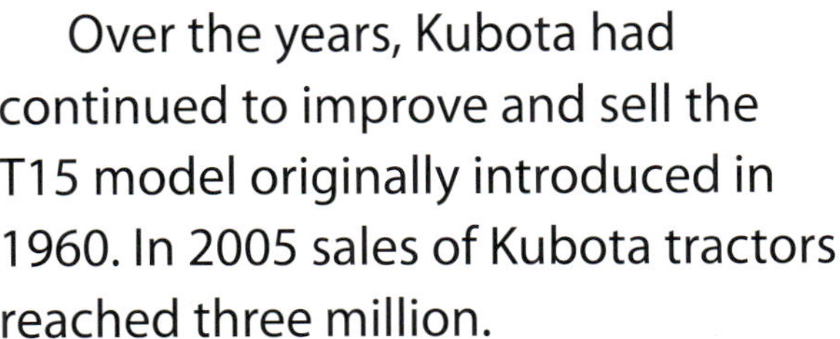

Over the years, Kubota had continued to improve and sell the T15 model originally introduced in 1960. In 2005 sales of Kubota tractors reached three million.

Today Kubota is known for its compact and subcompact tractors. Its compact tractors are the B and L series tractors. In 2020 Kubota introduced the B2401 compact tractor. This tractor is used for mowing lawns, light construction work, and landscaping.

Mahindra 575DI
AGROPANONKA

MAHINDRA

In 1945 brothers K. C. and J. C. Mahindra formed a company and began building light military vehicles in India. From there, the company grew. In 1963 it partnered with IH and began making tractors. The Mahindra B-275 was its first tractor. The company began selling tractors in the United States in 1994. By 2010 Mahindra was selling the most tractors of any company in the world. In the United States, Mahindra tractors are built in Texas, California, Tennessee, Pennsylvania, and Kansas. Mahindra sells subcompact, compact, and standard-size utility tractors.

Besides the tractors that carry the Mahindra name, the company also sells tractors under three other brand names. These brands are Swaraj, Mitsubishi, and Erkunt. These brands of Mahindra tractors are sold on six continents. In addition to tractors, Mahindra builds other farm equipment pulled by tractors. It produces combines and machines for planting rice.

Mahindra remains a popular tractor in India.

GLOBAL COMPANY

Mahindra tractors are popular in Asia, Africa, and South America. These tractors have a reputation for their fuel efficiency and strong pulling power. They have a horsepower range of 15 to 125. Swaraj tractors are popular in Bangladesh, Sri Lanka, Algeria, and Tanzania. These tractors have a horsepower range of 15 to 60.

Mitsubishi tractors are popular in the United States, Australia, Thailand, and South Korea. They have a compact design and are easy to operate. The Mitsubishi horsepower range is 13 to 135. Erkunt tractors are popular with farmers in Europe, the Middle East, and Africa. These tractors are built to work in both fields and orchards. The Erkunt horsepower range is 50 to 110.

Mitsubishi tractors are made in Japan.

MASSEY FERGUSON

In 1847 Daniel Massey opened a machine shop in Ontario, Canada, and named it the Massey Manufacturing Company. He had grown up on a farm and worked as a farmer himself. Then he opened the machine shop and began building

The steam-powered sawmill was used to cut lumber.

mechanical threshers. Farmers across Canada used these threshers for harvesting.

Around this same time, Alanson Harris opened a steam-powered sawmill and workshop in Ontario named A. Harris and Son. He began building farm equipment. Harris created the Brantford self-tying binder. This machine cut grain and tied it into bundles.

In 1891 the Massey Manufacturing Company and A. Harris and Son joined to form the Massey-Harris Company. Working together, the two companies offered the best products from both companies while sharing production and distribution costs. They could sell products at a cheaper price. By 1893 Massey-Harris was selling a wide range of farm equipment to farmers around the world.

Daniel Massey was born in 1798.

FOCUS ON TRACTORS

In the 1950s, Massey-Harris was known for its combines. Tractors were not its main focus. But in 1953, Harry Ferguson went to work at Massey-Harris. Ferguson had started building tractors soon after inventing the three-point hitch in the late 1920s. When Ferguson joined the company, it changed its name to Massey-Harris-Ferguson. The company began focusing on tractors.

Shortly after, it moved ahead of John Deere in tractor sales. It became the number two tractor company in the world in tractor sales, just behind IH. The company's name was shortened to Massey Ferguson in 1958.

In 1957 Massey Ferguson launched its MF 35 tractor. Before Massey and Ferguson merged to work together, this tractor was sold as the Ferguson FE35. It was the first in the combined company's MF series of tractors.

The MF 35 was built in Detroit, Michigan.

MASSEY · FERGUSON 35
FERGUSON SYSTEM
SUPERKING

In 1994 AGCO bought Massey Ferguson. AGCO continues to sell tractors and other farm equipment under the Massey Ferguson name. Today the company builds its farm equipment at plants in the United States and other countries around the world.

Massey Ferguson tractors range in size from subcompact models to higher horsepower row-crop tractors. Its subcompact tractors are the GC1700 series. Its compact tractors are the MF 2800 series. These tractors have plenty of engine power for light jobs around the farm. Besides their work performance, the tractors in the MF 2800 series have a comfortable cab, even when the farmer is working on rough land.

The company's standard-size utility tractors are designed with enough power to handle big farm jobs. These tractors include MF 5700 series. The row-crop tractors in the MF 8700 series are designed for heavy farm work on large farms, such as planting, plowing, harrowing, and weed control. These are the most powerful tractors Massey Ferguson has ever built, with up to 405 horsepower engines.

The Massey Ferguson 7720 sells for more than $150,000.

NEW HOLLAND

The New Holland company gets its name from New Holland, Pennsylvania. This is the town where Abe Zimmerman opened a machine repair shop in 1895. In 1903 Zimmerman founded the New Holland Machine Company, making farming equipment.

In 1947 Sperry Rand Corporation bought New Holland. The name changed to Sperry New Holland. Sperry New Holland was known for its combine machines. In 1975 the company introduced the twin-rotor design for combines. In this design, two rotors spin toward each other. Spirals called augers pull grain stalks to one end of the rotors. The stalks get sucked between the rotors. Bars along the rotors beat at the stalks, separating the grain from the stalks.

In a twin-rotor combine, grain stalks loop around the rotors several times to better separate grain.

Separated grain falls through mesh below the rotors. Tracks along the rotors guide the stalks to the other end, so stalks get multiple passes between the rotors. This separates more grain than the old combines with just one rotor, where the crops got only one pass. The twin-rotor design that Sperry New Holland invented is still used in combines today.

Combines are still sold under the New Holland name.

In 2022 CNH had more than 40,000 employees.

Ford bought Sperry New Holland in 1986. The name changed to Ford New Holland. A few years later, Fiat bought Ford New Holland and changed the name back to New Holland. In 1999 Fiat merged New Holland and Case Corporation. The new company was called CNH Global. It made tractors under the New Holland name.

TAKING ON TRACTORS

In 2002 New Holland entered the tractor business. Today it is known for its environmentally friendly tractors. New Holland started using biodiesel in all its engines in 2007. Biodiesel is a plant-based fuel that is better for the environment than fossil fuels. Fossil fuels can take millions of years to form, so the world has a limited supply of them. But because plants can constantly be grown, they are a renewable source. Biodiesel also releases less carbon dioxide into the air than fossil fuels.

New Holland introduced the world's first hydrogen-powered tractor, called the NH2, in 2009. Hydrogen-powered tractors are safer for the environment than traditional tractors. While traditional tractors release gases that are bad for the environment, hydrogen-powered tractors release water vapor. They are also easier to maintain and quieter than traditional tractors.

Although the NH2 was only a prototype and not for sale to the public, it showed New Holland's commitment to greener tractors.

New Holland advertises its methane-powered tractors as costing 30 percent less to run since they do not require traditional fuel.

In 2013 New Holland made a working prototype of a methane-powered tractor, which is fueled by animal waste. A methane-powered engine releases less greenhouse gas than engines powered by fossil fuels. This is because the gases from the animal waste would end up in the air either way. In 2019 New Holland launched the T6, the world's first totally methane-powered tractor. New Holland's T7 tractor, released in 2023, is a methane-powered tractor that uses fuel created from cow manure.

OLIVER

In the 1850s, James Oliver began building iron plows in Indiana. In 1868 he named his business South Bend Iron Works. In addition to plows, it made parts for sewing machines and wagons. By the 1870s, Oliver had 200 employees and needed a bigger factory. In 1881 Oliver had 900 employees and was making 600 plows a day.

In 1901 the business changed its name to Oliver Chilled Plow Works. Its slogan was "Plowmakers for the World." James Oliver died in 1908, but his son and grandson took over the business.

James Oliver lived in South Bend, Indiana, in the Oliver Mansion.

Oliver plows were used in Scotland in 1919, including at demonstrations.

When Henry Ford began making the Fordson tractor, he hired the Oliver company to make all Fordson plows. In the 1920s, when Ford began to focus more on cars than tractors, Oliver started building its own tractors. It called its first tractor the Oliver Chilled Plow Tractor.

TRACTOR EQUIPMENT

After Oliver made its first tractor, it realized it needed to expand the business to include more farm equipment. In 1929 Oliver merged with Hart-Parr, Nichols & Shepard, and the American Seeding Company. The new company was called Oliver Farm Equipment Company. It produced tractors as well as tools for tilling, planting, and harvesting. In 1944 the name changed to the Oliver Corporation.

During the 1940s Oliver built more than farm machines. It built airplane, tank, and gun parts for the US military. It also built crane carriers for the US Army Corps of Engineers.

In 1960 White Motor Corporation bought the Oliver Corporation. The last tractor that carried the Oliver name was the 2255 model, built in 1976. After that, the tractors carried the White name. The factories that had built the Oliver tractors for years were closed. Today Oliver tractors are owned by people who collect and restore antique tractors.

In the 1930s, Oliver sold tractors with tiptoe wheels, which had metal parts sticking out from the main wheel to grip the ground.

SAME

The Italian company SAME was started in 1942 by two brothers, Francesco and Eugenio Cassani. Their father owned a farm machine shop. The brothers began working in their father's shop as teenagers. They learned to build and repair farm machines. Around 1922 they began building a diesel engine. This type of

engine was relatively new at this time. In 1927 the brothers built one of the world's first diesel-engine tractors. It won first place in an agricultural competition in Rome, Italy.

For a number of years, the brothers pursued other engine projects and business ventures. Then in 1942, the brothers founded SAME. SAME is an acronym for Società Accomandita Motori Endotermici (Endothermic Engines Limited Partnership). SAME first built diesel engines and repaired military vehicles. In about 1946 SAME began building a motorized three-wheel mower. Then the brothers noticed that tractors were gaining popularity and changing farm life in the United Kingdom. In 1948 SAME began building tractors.

In 1984 Italy sold stamps that featured a SAME tractor called the Galaxy.

COMPANY EXPANSION

In 1952 the company launched its DA series tractor. This was the first standard tractor in the world to use four-wheel drive. In 1966 SAME introduced a tractor called the Centauro. The Centauro tractors were made in 55, 60, and 65 horsepower versions. Ten years later, SAME launched the more powerful Buffalo tractor. It came in 120 and 130 horsepower versions.

SAME bought a Swiss tractor company in 1979. The two joined to become the Gruppo SLH, or SLH Group. SLH became the second-largest Italian company making tractors. In 1995 SLH bought a German farm machine company. It became SAME Deutz-Fahr, or SDF Group. SAME remained one of its brands.

SAME tractors have been sold in many countries, including the United Kingdom.

Tractors that are built for vineyards and orchards are sometimes called specialized tractors.

TRACTOR VARIETY

In 1991 SAME launched the Frutteto II tractor. The company designed this compact tractor for use in orchards and vineyards. SAME continues to build tractors designed for orchards, vineyards, and olive groves. These include several in the Frutteto series and the Explorer TB.

Oranges are among the fruits that grow on trees in orchards. They are harvested between October and June.

SAME also sells several tractors for use in open fields. These tractor series include the Explorer, Laser, Dorado, and Tiger. SAME introduced the Explorer tractor in 1983. The Explorer is versatile for use on large and small farms, and it is easy to operate. It has become one of SAME's most popular tractors. The company has sold more than 130,000 Explorers. The Laser is designed for use in a wide range of farm jobs around the world. The Dorado is a general-purpose tractor that can also be used in widely spaced fruit orchards or vineyards. The Tiger is an all-purpose tractor with a more compact design, built for a variety of jobs on small farms.

SAME makes a small tractor called the Solaris. This tractor is designed for use in tight spaces such as greenhouses or nurseries. The Solaris works well for crops that grow low to the ground. SAME also sells Krypton tractors. These tractors have tracks instead of wheels.

The SAME Solaris 45 was released in 1999.

Sonalika exports tractors to more than 100 countries.

SONALIKA

Sonalika is an Indian tractor company started in 1996 by Lachman Das Mittal. Mittal started the Sonalika Group after retiring at age 65 from his job with an insurance company. Mittal later retired from Sonalika, but his sons and grandsons run the business. The name *Sonalika* means "lines of gold" in Hindi and is the name of a variety of wheat. Sonalika's tractor plant in Hoshiarpur, India, is the world's largest tractor plant.

Threshers were the first farm equipment that Sonalika built. After several years of success selling threshers, the company started building tractors. Besides tractors, Sonalika produces many other pieces of equipment for farm use. They include combines, potato planters, balers, and straw reapers.

TRACTOR MODELS

Sonalika's DI 745 tractors are built for farms that are small and medium in size. These general-purpose tractors perform a wide range of jobs. Sonalika's DI 750 tractors are built for heavy-duty jobs. They have strong pulling power. The DI 60 tractors are built for larger farm operations. The DI 60 tills, plants, and harvests large fields. Sonalika's compact DI 35 tractor is built for use in tight spaces on small farms and in orchards.

The Sonalika DI 60 tractor was released in 2006.

In 2021 Sonalika introduced the Tiger Electric tractor. It was the first electric tractor produced in India. Electric tractors are safer for the environment than traditional tractors because they give off less pollution. They also need less maintenance than tractors with a traditional diesel motor.

Sonalika also makes tractors that work in rice paddies. Farmers till rice paddies while they are flooded with water. This work is called puddling. Sonalika's Mahabali tractors are built for puddling. Tractors built for this work generally have very wide tires and four-wheel drive that helps them grip wet soil. The engines are usually 30 to 50 horsepower and built to function in very wet conditions. Sonalika is now the third-largest tractor company in India. It is the number-one brand of tractors exported from India to other countries.

Rice is a major crop in Asia. It is grown in flooded fields called paddies.

People can fly drones over crops to spray pesticides. This can replace the need for a small plane or helicopter to do the same job.

AGRICULTURAL DRONES

Agricultural drones are unmanned aerial vehicles (UAVs) that carry sensors and cameras. Drones help farmers with a variety of tasks. Using drones, farmers can track the health of their crops, map their fields, and monitor the weather. They can collect soil and water samples, count livestock, and apply pesticides. A farmer can see the data and images the drone gathers on a tablet or computer.

Farmers have used flying machines since the early 1900s. In 1906 a farmer in New Zealand used a hot-air balloon to

spread grass seed over his land. Then planes left over from World War I were turned into crop dusters. These planes flew over fields to apply insecticide on crops. From the air, farmers could accomplish some tasks more efficiently than while riding on a tractor or walking.

DRONES IN FARMING

The first reports of people using cameras attached to drones that looked like model aircraft for farm work happened around 1985. Drones became much more popular for farm use in the early 2000s, when they became more affordable. As the prices have dropped, drone use in farming has quickly risen.

Agricultural drones can have tanks, pumps, and nozzles to store and spray pesticides.

BayWa and Naïo Technologies invented a robot called Dino, which can weed fields.

AGRICULTURAL ROBOTS

Agricultural robots are autonomous machines used on farms for a wide range of jobs. They are sometimes called agribots. Robot jobs include harvesting, sorting and packing, and pulling weeds. Robots are also used to mow, prune, or spray crops. These machines can work quickly and accurately.

FUNCTION

Building robots that are effective for farm work is not easy. A robot that picks or sorts needs an arm that can gently but firmly grasp a vegetable or fruit tree. If the robotic arm is too gentle, it leaves crops behind. If it is too rough, it damages the crop. Companies that make farm robots are always working to improve them so that they work more effectively.

At times when farmers struggle to find workers, robots can be a great solution. Robots can work around the clock. A single person can supervise a whole squad of robots, significantly increasing productivity.

Cattle farms can use robots made by a company called Lely to push feed closer to cattle.

When an operator used a lever on the Allen Scythe's handles, the engine would turn the wheels so the operator did not have to push it.

ALLEN SCYTHES

A scythe is a hand tool with a long blade used to cut grasses or crops. The Allen Scythe is a machine that cuts tall, rough grasses or crops using two blades with sharp teeth. One blade shifts side-to-side to overlap with the other blade, similar to how electric

clippers or modern hedge trimmers work. The machine looks like a lawn mower.

HISTORY

The machine was built by John Allen & Sons in England starting in 1935. Allen Scythes were popular with small farm owners. These farmers might not have been able to afford a tractor. But the Allen Scythe was useful beyond cutting grass.

Farmers attached small trailers to an Allen Scythe. They also used the Allen Scythe to power or pull attachments such as plows, sheep clippers, and water sprayers. Even though the Allen Scythe has not been produced since 1973, some people still use the old machines.

The handheld scythe is the inspiration for the Allen Scythe's name. The user holds the scythe's handle and swings it with the blade low to the ground to cut tall grass.

The UTV is also called a side-by-side (SxS).

ALL-TERRAIN VEHICLES (ATVS)

Farmers use all-terrain vehicles (ATVs) and utility task vehicles (UTVs) for a variety of tasks. The ATV, also called a quad or four-wheeler, is built for a single rider. The UTV is bigger and has room for two to four riders. ATVs and UTVs can reach an average top speed of approximately 50 miles per hour (80 kmh).

USES

Farmers use these off-road vehicles to move items such as bales of hay, feed bags, or seed. The ATV can typically carry about 100 pounds (45 kg) of cargo in the front and 200 pounds (90 kg) in the back. The bigger UTVs can carry up to 1,000 pounds (450 kg) of cargo. A variety of attachments for ATVs and UTVs are used to spread seed or fertilizer on fields.

Farmers can use ATVs and UTVs while herding animals or building fences. They haul fence supplies with the vehicle. Farmers can even attach a device on the back of the vehicle that helps unwind fence wiring.

An ATV can be useful when ranchers must travel long distances to find and gather their animals.

BALERS

A baler cuts crops and shapes them into bales. Farmers use a tractor to pull the baler. Farmers use it for crops such as hay, straw, cotton, and flax. Sometimes the farmer cuts the crop and leaves it on the field in long rows called windrows to dry before it is baled. If it is baled while too moist, the crop can spoil. Once the baler shapes the cut crops into bales, those bales can be easily stored or transported to other locations.

Balers make bundles of straw or other crop materials that are easy to transport.

TYPES

There are round balers and rectangular balers. The round baler produces rolled bales in the shape of cylinders. The rectangular baler produces rectangular bales. After cutting and shaping the crop, the baler fastens twine or netting around the bale to hold it securely.

As an added step, some farmers use a bale wrapper to wrap plastic around the bale. If the crop is stored outside, the plastic wrapping helps keep out moisture that might spoil the crop. Case IH, John Deere, Massey Ferguson, and New Holland are some of the companies that produce balers in the United States.

Round balers were developed later than rectangular balers, with the technology to make large, round bales first emerging in the 1970s.

The buck rake, *front*, is also called a sweep rake, bull rake, hay buck, or hay sweep.

BUCK RAKES

A buck rake is used to gather cut hay from the field and move it to the barn. Once hay is cut, farmers leave it on the field to dry in windrows. Then the buck rake's tongs help it scoop up the cut hay. Farmers can then pile the hay in a barn for storage.

HISTORY

The buck rake was invented in the late 1800s. Horses or mules pulled early buck rakes. Later, farmers attached buck rakes to tractors, cars, or trucks. Some companies also made self-propelled buck rakes. Occasionally farmers even built their own. Using wood and steel, they made a large, simple rake and attached it to a car or truck. Today other machines and tools help farmers gather hay. But some farmers still use buck rakes.

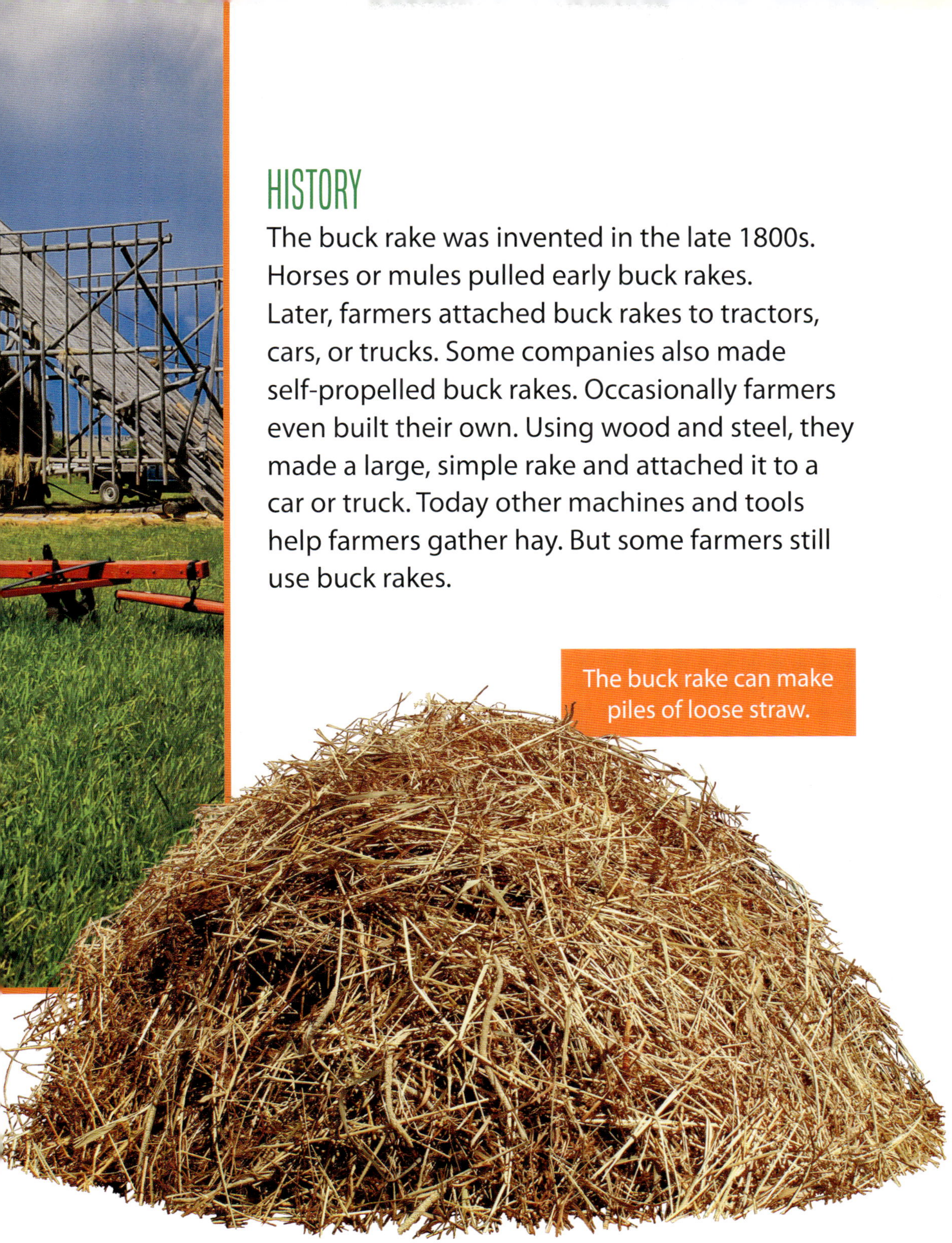

The buck rake can make piles of loose straw.

Combines can be used to harvest wheat. Some combines can be adjusted to handle various crops.

COMBINES

The combine is a machine that harvests grain crops. It is called a combine because it combines several harvesting tasks into one. This one machine cuts, sorts, and cleans the grain. Like the tractor, the invention of the combine had a major impact on farm life. With this machine, the farmer could do more work in less time with fewer workers.

In some crops, such as wheat, the grain that is useful for food grows at the top of the plant. Before the combine was invented, farmers cut stalks of grain crops by hand with a scythe. Then they separated the grain from the stalk by beating the cut stalks. This part of the process was called threshing. After that step, the farmer had to clean out any debris left with the grain.

HISTORY

The combine was invented in Scotland. Reverend Patrick Bell made a reaper machine in 1826. It used something like scissors to cut the grain stalks. A short while later, American inventors Hiram Moore and John Hascall developed a combine-thresher. Horses or mules pulled this machine.

Most combines are at least 11 feet (3.4 m) tall.

A team of 20 mules pulls a combine in Washington State in 1941.

Moore and Hascall's combine had many of the same features as today's combines. It had a blade to cut the plant stalks. Then a reel moved the grain onto a platform. From the platform, the grain was pushed into the threshing cylinder, where it was separated from the plant. Screens and fans cleaned the grain. Farmers used as many as 30 horses or mules to pull the combine.

By the 1880s, inventors added a steam engine that powered the moving parts of the combine. But animals still had to pull the combine. Combines pulled by tractors came into use in the 1920s. Combines became more widely used in the 1930s. Before the combine was invented, it took a team of about 20 to 30 workers to thresh grain. But only four or five workers were needed to operate a combine doing the same job. By 1937 farmers could buy the first self-propelled combines. No tractors were needed to pull them.

A Massey-Harris combine from the 1920s was pulled by a tractor.

The spout that dumps grain from a combine into a grain cart is called an auger spout.

COMBINES TODAY

Today farmers use combines to harvest cereal crops such as wheat, corn, barley, oats, and rye. They also harvest sunflower seeds, soybeans, cotton, and flax with the combines. Equipment on the machines helps the farmer measure how much crop is being harvested. A container on the combine called a hopper holds the harvested crop until it can be moved to a grain cart. Today's combines have either large tires or tracks. They can move through a field harvesting the crop in sections more than 40 feet (12 m) wide.

COTTON HARVESTERS

The cotton harvester gathers cotton from the cotton plant. The mature fruit of the cotton plant is the cotton boll. The round cotton boll consists of separate chambers that hold the seeds and fuzzy white fibers. John Rust from Arkansas patented the first cotton harvester in 1933. In the late 1940s, companies began producing cotton harvesters for farmers to buy.

The cotton boll protects the seeds within it and helps the seeds spread as the wind catches the fibers.

TYPES

There are two basic types of cotton harvesters. The stripper-type harvester removes leaves, stems, and cotton bolls from the plant. The stripper uses two rollers to gather the cotton, which is moved to a large basket on the harvester. Then the cotton is packed into bales. Cotton bales can be wrapped in a protective covering like other crop bales.

Picker-type harvesters remove the cotton from the open boll. Most of the plant is left behind in the field. Slender rods called spindles are attached to a large drum. The spindles and drum turn. As they turn, the cotton fiber wraps around the spindles. A device called a doffer removes the cotton from the spindles. The doffer places it in a large basket on the harvester.

Stripper-type cotton harvesters, *right*, are easier to maintain than picker-types, *left*.

The cups on a milker have rubber or silicone liners that help make a seal.

COW MILKING MACHINES

The milking machine extracts milk from a cow. The machine has cups that attach to a cow's four teats. The cups are connected to tubes that bring the milk to a container. In order for the machine to work properly, the cups must be attached securely so that there is a seal. The machine's pump then creates a vacuum within the tubes. It makes a vacuum, eases the vacuum, and makes another vacuum in pulses, sucking the milk out of the cow's teats and through the tubes.

HISTORY

Milking cows by hand takes a lot of time and energy. So in the 1800s, various inventors patented vacuum milking machines. Unlike modern milking machines, which are powered by electricity, these early machines created a constant vacuum with hand pumps. The machines worked, but they were uncomfortable for cows. The pulsator, patented in 1898, solved this problem. It worked by varying the amount of pressure on the teat, giving it time to rest between vacuum pulses. Pulsators are still a feature of milking machines today.

Some milking systems are on a rotating platform. This allows cattle to load up, and as the platform rotates, workers can attach the milkers to each cow as it passes by.

CULTIPACKERS

A cultipacker helps a farmer prepare a field for planting seeds. The farmer uses a tractor or an ATV to pull the machine. Farmers began using cultipackers in the early 1900s.

The ridges on a cultipacker can be different shapes and sizes depending on the brand.

HOW THEY WORK

A farmer uses a cultipacker after a field has been plowed but before the seeds are planted. The cultipacker has large rollers that smooth the soil, making the ground more level. As its name reflects, this tool packs the soil, but not too tightly. The rollers have ridges that break up small clumps of dirt and squeeze out air pockets in the soil.

After this is done, the farmer sows the seeds. This involves scattering the seeds onto the soil either by hand or with a broadcast spreader. Sometimes farmers use the cultipacker again after the seeds are sown to press them into the soil. This ensures that the seeds are firmly touching the soil but not pressed too far down. If the seed has good contact with the soil, it has a better chance of growing. If it is pressed in too deeply, it cannot grow. Today's cultipackers come in several sizes. Farmers use them on both smaller garden plots and large fields.

Small cultipackers are made for ATVs, and very large ones are used with tractors. Large cultipackers can be 10 feet (3 m) or longer.

Pickup trucks can pull different kinds of trailers.

FARM TRUCKS

Farmers use many kinds of trucks in their work. With a pickup truck, farmers can move supplies or tools. They can tow trailers carrying animals. If the truck has four-wheel drive, the farmer can use it on muddy or snow-covered land.

HISTORY

Historians credit Henry Ford with building the first pickup truck. Ford saw farmers using Ford Model T cars for farm work.

The farmers modified the cars, adding a cargo box on the back. So Ford built the Model T Roadster with Pickup Body in 1925.

Over the years, pickup trucks have changed. The cabs and beds can be bigger. The cabs can seat more people. The engines are more powerful. Pickups remain popular vehicles for both farmers and everyday drivers. More than three million pickups were sold in the United States in 2020.

Farmers use other kinds of trucks too. Larger trucks such as semitrucks and trailers move farmers' livestock or harvested crops from the farm to the marketplace. Some farmers own these large trucks. Others might hire a trucking company for this type of work.

Semitruck trailers used for hauling livestock need many holes so the animals can get fresh air.

Grain carts are also called auger carts or chaser bins.

GRAIN CARTS

A grain cart transports harvested grain from a combine to a truck or wagon near the field. Grain carts have large tires or tracks. They can be pulled easily in muddy fields.

HOW THEY WORK

The tractor pulling the grain cart drives alongside the combine. Moving side by side, the combine continues harvesting grain while also loading the harvested grain from its hopper to the grain cart. This process requires good communication between the drivers of the combine and the tractor pulling the grain cart. When the combine driver has emptied the harvested grain from the hopper onto the cart, the grain cart can move it to a truck waiting near the field. Using a grain cart allows the farmer to work more efficiently. The combine can continue running without stopping while the grain cart moves the loads of grain off the field.

A full grain cart transfers the grain into a semitruck trailer, which will transport the grain to a grain dryer.

GRAIN DRYERS

Machines called grain dryers help farmers dry harvested crops. Some crops contain so much moisture that they can start to

Grain dryers use a lot of energy. Keeping them well-maintained and thoroughly cleaned can help reduce energy use.

mold before they completely air dry. This mold would make the grain unsafe for humans or animals to eat. Grains that are properly dried before being stored will last longer and have a better quality. Corn and soybeans are two crops that usually need to be dried by machine.

Because grain crops are sold by weight, they need to be dried to a certain moisture percentage. That way buyers know exactly how much grain they are getting in the load they are buying. The US government has determined the best moisture levels for crops to make them safe for storage and then later for eating. When a farmer brings corn or soybeans to market, a probe is placed in the grain to measure the moisture. If the moisture level is too high, the farmer gets a lower price for the grain.

TYPES

Farmers use different kinds of grain dryers. Some dryers push heated air through the grain with large fans. Other dryers use a spiral blade called an auger, which rotates, moving the grain around until it is evenly dried.

Companies may have several grain dryers so they can handle a large volume of grain.

Augers in a grinder-mixer can both cut and mix feed.

GRINDER-MIXERS

The grinder-mixer grinds and mixes the grain for livestock feed. Grinding grain makes it easier for animals to digest. Corn, wheat, soybeans, and barley are some common grains ground for animal feed.

METHODS

Farmers began making machines to crush grain in the late 1800s. Grinder-mixers can use different methods to break up grain. Hammer grinders crush grain with a high-speed hammer. Counter-roller grinders use rotating rollers to crush grain. Claw grinders use rotating prongs that crush the grain as they turn.

Farmers may choose a grinder based on the grains they need to crush. Veterinarians and farmers work to determine the best size for the grains fed to animals. The grinder-mixer can be a stand-alone machine or a machine pulled by a tractor.

Farmers might make chicken feed by grinding and mixing corn, soybeans, vitamins, and other ingredients.

On small farms, tractors dig up root vegetables after a haulm topper has removed the stems.

HAULM TOPPERS

A haulm topper prepares root crops for harvesting. Root crops are foods that grow underground, such as potatoes, beets, carrots, garlic, onions, and peanuts. The haulm topper cuts off plant stalks while the root vegetables are still in the ground. The word *haulm* means "stalk" or "stem." Once the haulm topper cuts the stalk, the crops can then be more easily harvested from the soil. The haulm topper can be mounted on the front or back of a tractor.

PAIRING EQUIPMENT

Farmers sometimes use the haulm topper along with a potato harvester. They attach the haulm topper to the front of the tractor. The potato harvester is attached to the back of the tractor. As the farmer drives the tractor through the field, the haulm topper cuts away the stalk. Then the harvester lifts the potatoes out of the soil and drops them onto a web that shakes away the soil.

Root plants, such as beets, grow with the main edible portion underground, while the stalks and leaves grow aboveground.

Rotary rakes spin the rake teeth at an angle so they push hay to one side and then lift up to avoid pushing it farther.

HAY RAKES

A hay rake pushes hay into rows. After the hay has dried, the baler picks it up. A tractor pulls the hay rake. Farmers can choose from several hay rakes, depending on the job.

TYPES

Rotary rakes have several arms extending from a central point. Metal teeth come down from the ends of the arms. The arms spin in a circle. The teeth catch the hay in the front of the machine, scooping it sideways. As the teeth with the hay reach the back of the machine, they lift into the air to stop pushing the hay. This leaves the hay in a windrow.

The bar rake has a cylinder of bars with short metal fingers. The cylinder is at an angle behind the tractor. The cylinder spins, raking the hay toward the far end into a windrow. This is one of the oldest rake designs.

Bar rakes have been used for more than 100 years.

Wheel rakes with two arms can push hay to a central point behind the tractor.

Some wheel rakes have one arm positioned at an angle behind the tractor. Others are shaped like an arrow. Two arms extend forward from a point behind the tractor. Wheels on the arms push hay back toward the farthest point, making a windrow.

The belt rake has a series of metal-tooth rakes attached to a belt. The belt is positioned perpendicular to the tractor. The belt rotates so that the rakes at the bottom of the belt scoop hay to one side of the tractor's path.

HYDROPONIC EQUIPMENT

Hydroponics is a method of farming without soil. This kind of farming gets its name from two Greek words. *Hydro* means "water." *Ponos* means "labor." Farmers add nutrients to the water for healthy plant growth. They can grow herbs, vegetables, and fruits using hydroponics.

Hydroponics is also called nutriculture, soilless culture, or tank farming.

Hydroponic trays have holes that let roots hang into the water but keep the plants from falling through.

SYSTEMS

There are several hydroponic farming systems. In some systems, the plant roots are in water. Other systems use a soil substitute, such as peat moss, coconut fiber, or clay pebbles. Plants are grown in large containers that hold water, nutrients, and the soil substitute. If the farmer is growing plants in water with no soil substitute, a pump adds air to the water.

Hydroponic systems can be built for use indoors or outdoors. Indoor systems use lights to help the plants grow. The lights give the plants the wavelengths of light energy they need while eliminating the light wavelengths not absorbed by

the plants. Sensors ensure plants get the proper amounts of water, nutrients, and light.

Because the plants grow in a controlled environment, farmers do not need to use as many pesticides and herbicides to control pests and diseases. This is healthier for humans, animals, and the environment. Hydroponic farming can be done year-round indoors. It can also be done in areas where the soil is contaminated and unsafe for growing crops.

Indoor hydroponic systems need a lot of light bulbs to simulate the sun.

Land imprinters are used in places that have experienced desertification, which means that human activity in a dry area has caused the vegetation to decrease significantly.

LAND IMPRINTERS

A land imprinter is a large, heavy roller with ridges. Farmers use the land imprinter to plant seeds in dry ground where it is difficult for plants to take root and grow. A tractor or other large vehicle pulls the machine. As the roller moves, it forms small impressions in the soil. Afterward, the field looks something like a giant checkerboard, with a pattern of indentations in the soil.

Some imprinters include a seed box that distributes the seeds as the imprinter rolls across the soil. When seeds are spread across the imprinted soil, they have a better chance of taking root and growing. The impressions then give the young plants some shelter from rain, wind, and sunlight.

HISTORY

Robert Dixon built the first land imprinter in 1976. He continued improving the machines for several decades. Dixon's land imprinters are credited with successfully seeding thousands of acres of dry, sandy soil in Arizona.

Land imprinters can help ranchers plant grass in desert soil so their cattle can graze.

Approximately 80 percent of nutrients in manure is available to plants the season after application. More becomes available in later seasons as the waste breaks down.

MANURE SPREADERS

A tractor pulls a manure spreader to deposit manure over a field. Manure is organic material used to fertilize crops. It consists of animal feces and urine. Sometimes straw, sawdust, or hay is mixed in with the animal waste. Manure has nitrogen, phosphorus, and potassium, which are nutrients that help plants grow. Farmers use cow, horse, and chicken manure because they have good levels of each of these nutrients for plant growth. Manure also helps the soil absorb water.

TYPES

Different spreaders are used for dry manure and liquid manure. Dry, solid manure is spread from a trailer that the tractor pulls. Turning parts on the trailer break up the manure and spread it evenly on the ground. A slurry spreader is used to apply liquid manure. Liquid manure is spread onto the soil or injected into the soil. With both the dry and liquid manure, farmers can control how much manure is applied to an area.

Manure is considered dry if it is at least 20 percent solid waste.

Very large mowers can handle tall grass over a wide area.

MOWERS

A mower cuts grasses and other crops to be gathered for animal feed. Mowers can be pulled by tractors or be self-propelled. A mower has blades that cut the crops close to the ground. The three main types of mowers are sickle bar mowers, disc mowers, and drum mowers.

TYPES

Before tractors were invented, horses pulled the sickle bar mower. Triangle-shaped blades cut the crops. Today this mower is useful for a farmer driving a small, lightweight tractor.

Disc mowers have small discs, and each disc has sharp blades attached. The discs spin at high speed so the blades can cut the crop. These mowers generally require a hydraulic tractor so that the mower can be lifted and lowered when needed.

Drum mowers have been popular in Europe. In recent years, they have gained popularity among farmers in the United States. They have two large drums that turn. A large disc with blades is attached to each drum. The drums rotate, and the discs and blades rotate with them. The drums' weight provides more power to cut through dense areas of growth.

Riding lawn mowers can be used on farmyards, but they are also used on suburban and urban lawns.

The planter carries fertilizer in large tanks.

PLANTERS

A tractor pulls a planter, which sows seeds. The planter breaks open the soil and precisely deposits the seeds at a set depth. The machine then covers the planted seed with soil. A planter can typically seed between two and 48 rows, depending on the model. It can also carry fertilizer to provide nutrition to the newly deposited seeds. The fastest planters drive at about 10 miles per hour (16 kmh).

The planter places the seeds in tidy hills or rows. It can plant both small and large seeds. Buyers can select from different row spacing options. When seeds are planted by hand, some seeds might be placed too shallow or too deep. The planter places seeds at an even, consistent depth, so farmers get a better harvest. Some planters plant young crops instead of seeds.

Sunflowers need to be planted at least 0.5 inches (1.3 cm) in the ground with at least 2 feet (0.6 m) between each row.

Disc plows have a series of discs lined up so they cut into the ground.

PLOWS

Farmers use plows to break up soil to prepare the soil for planting. Discs or knives attached to the plow cut the soil as a tractor pulls the plow across the field. Early plows were iron tools pulled by horses or oxen. When tractors were invented in the early 1900s, farmers adjusted their plows so tractors could pull them.

TYPES

Over time, plows have become more specialized. Disc plows use metal plates to cut the soil. They are useful in hard or rocky soil. Rotary plows use long, curved blades. The rotary plow also works well in hard soil. Subsoiler and chisel plows are used to break up packed soil. They can break the soil to depths of 3 feet (0.9 m), deeper than other plows. The subsoiler has a couple of shanks, which are heavy steel blades that allow it to cut into the soil deeply. It does not turn over soil. Chisel plows are similar but have many more shanks.

Rotary plows are sometimes called tillers or rototillers.

One farmer drives the tractor while another farmer operates the reaper-binder.

REAPER-BINDERS

The reaper-binder is used to harvest and bind crops. It can be pulled by a tractor or be self-propelled. Farmers typically use reaper-binders for crops such as wheat, rice, grass, barley, oats, and straw.

Before the reaper-binder was invented, harvesting grain crops was a slow process done by hand. Farmers cut grain using a sickle or scythe. The sickle has a more rounded blade, and the scythe has a straighter blade. A worker using a sickle and a cradle, which caught the cut grain and dropped it into a neat row, could harvest about 2 acres (0.8 ha) a day.

With the invention of the reaper, a worker could harvest 12 to 15 acres (5 to 6 ha) a day.

HISTORY

In the early 1800s, several inventors were working to invent reapers. In about 1830, Cyrus McCormick invented a horse-pulled reaper. The reaper cut stalks of grain. The farmer then hand tied the grain into bundles. At the same time, Wisconsin jeweler Charles Baxter Withington was building a binder that fastened grain together using wire. Withington and McCormick put their inventions together to make the reaper-binder. Sales of the machine rose quickly.

To use a handheld sickle, a worker grabs a clump of grass, pulls it tight, and then cuts it near the ground.

The husk, *bottom*, protects the rice grain as it grows.

RICE MILLING MACHINES

When rice is harvested, the rice grain is covered in a husk. Before rice can be eaten, the husk must be removed. This process of removing the husk is called rice milling. Rice milling machines do this job.

PROCESS

The first step in rice milling is cleaning. The machine removes dust, clay, sand, and stones. Next, the rice passes across rough surfaces in the machine, which break off the husks. At this point, the farmer has brown rice that can be eaten.

To get white rice, the milling process continues. The machine removes the brown layer by rubbing the grains together while applying pressure between a roller and a leather pad. This polishing produces white rice.

The white rice is then parboiled. In this step, the rice is soaked in vitamin water and heated with steam or boiling water. The step makes the rice more nutritious. After parboiling, the rice is dried and packaged for sale. Some more advanced rice mills use lasers to sort out the broken or immature rice kernels from the good rice.

After milling, rice can be packaged in bulk bags.

The rock picker is sometimes called a destoner, rock windrower, or rock rake.

ROCK PICKERS

Rock pickers remove rocks from soil. Too many rocks in the soil cause problems for farmers. Large rocks can make it challenging for farmers to plant seeds or harvest crops. Rocks can also damage farm equipment. Rock pickers are pushed or towed by a tractor. The pickers can also be fastened to the front of bulldozers.

HISTORY

In the early 1940s, Canadian farmer Peter Anderson invented the first mechanical rock picker. Rock pickers can work in a few ways. Some collect rocks, working like a giant dustpan and broom. They sweep rocks into a basket. When the farmer finishes pulling the rock picker over a field, the basket of rocks can be dumped. Other rock pickers scoop the rocks into a slotted basket. The slots allow the soil to fall back to the ground while holding the rocks to be discarded.

Rocks that get pulled from a field can be used to make a stone fence.

SEED DRILLS

A seed drill sows seeds into the ground. The machine places the seeds at a precise depth. With the seed drill, the farmer can control the spacing between seeds as well as the planting depth. By planting seeds at the best depth for a particular crop, the crops are more likely to grow well.

The seed drill is similar to the planter. But the planter can place the seeds in hills and rows, while the seed drill cannot. The seed drill is better suited for planting small seeds.

Seed drills have tubes that move the seeds from the main bucket to a part called the share, which drops the seeds into the ground.

A single horse could pull a seed drill that planted one row at a time.

HISTORY

Thousands of years ago, farmers used a tube and a plow to plant seeds in Mesopotamia, which today is Iraq and parts of several other countries. This device was likely one of the earliest seed drills. In 1701 Jethro Tull's seed drill was the first agricultural machine with moving parts. Tull used a plow in front that created a row in the soil. A funnel dropped the seed into the soil. A harrow then covered the seed with soil. Tull's first seed drill planted just one row at a time. His later designs were horse-pulled drills that could plant several rows at a time.

The self-loading wagon cuts and loads grass from its front.

SELF-LOADING WAGONS

A self-loading wagon cuts and loads grasses onto a large wagon pulled by a tractor. The self-loading wagon has blades to cut the grass. Turning rotors move the cut grasses into the wagon. A self-loading wagon can pick up grasses that were cut earlier and left on the field to dry.

HISTORY

The work of cutting and gathering cut grasses once required a farmer and tractor, as well as other helpers and trucks. With a self-loading wagon, one farmer with a tractor can do that work alone. A self-loading wagon can cut a farmer's labor costs by approximately 50 percent.

Farm equipment companies have produced self-loading wagons since the 1960s. These wagons have been popular with farmers in Europe and Canada for many years. In Canada these wagons are commonly used by dairy farmers. The wagons are gaining popularity with American farmers.

The self-loading wagon doesn't always cut grass. It sometimes only picks up windrows of grass.

Traditional sprayers, *pictured*, apply chemicals without the control maintained by smart sprayers.

SMART SPRAYERS

A smart sprayer allows a farmer to precisely apply herbicides and pesticides to crops. Weeds compete with crops for water, nutrients, and sunlight. Weeds can also carry pests and diseases that might attack the crops.

TARGETING WEEDS

While herbicides and pesticides are effective in controlling weeds and pests, they present some challenges. They can sometimes damage crops. They are also harmful to the microorganisms in the soil, making the soil less productive for crop growth. Some chemicals are harmful to humans and animals living on or near the farm. And much of the sprayed chemicals never reach the weeds or pests. They may land on the soil or healthy crops or be washed away by rainwater. Smart sprayers can apply just the right amount of the chemicals.

Burdock is a common weed that grows in fields.

Cameras on smart sprayers can see weeds that farmers probably wouldn't spot.

Smart sprayers use cameras and artificial intelligence to apply the herbicide more precisely. The sprayer system has images of all the plants the sprayer might encounter. Using artificial intelligence, the system knows the difference between crops and weeds. The software tells the sprayer precisely where to spray, targeting the weeds and avoiding the crops. The smart sprayer cuts down the amount of herbicide used, making it safer for people, animals, and the environment.

SORTERS

A sorter is used to sort fruits, vegetables, grains, and nuts. The sorting can be done by size, weight, shape, or color.

Some sorting machines can separate seeds used for planting.

HOW THEY WORK

A crop being sorted moves through the sorting machine on a conveyor belt. Sorters use high-quality cameras to quickly inspect the crop. The cameras are programmed to look for specific details, depending on what crop is being sorted. The cameras check for differences in size or color. They look for rotten produce or foreign materials.

Sorting crops is an important step in preparing them for the market.

Chicken eggs can be sorted. Machines and human workers sort eggs by sex so people who want hens to lay eggs can purchase only female eggs.

Sorters can also be programmed to look for foods damaged by diseases or parasites. The produce drops into a large container. When the cameras detect fruits or vegetables of poor quality, levers knock those items into a different container mid-fall.

In a similar way, seed sorters provide the farmer with the best-quality seeds. If a farmer plants more high-quality seeds, the harvest is likely to produce better crops. Seed sorters can be used with even very small seeds, such as onion, lettuce, or carrot seeds.

STRIP-TILL TOOLBARS

A tractor pulls a strip-till toolbar to cultivate the soil. The strip-till toolbar loosens only the narrow band of soil needed for planting. It leaves most of the past season's crop stubble covering the ground. When wind and rain come, stubble protects the soil, reducing soil erosion. The stubble also helps keep moisture in the soil.

The strip-till toolbar is also called a strip-till cultivator.

Crop stubble lies in the undisturbed rows of a strip-tilled field.

The machine keeps a healthy level of microorganism activity in the soil because most of the soil is left undisturbed. This contributes to healthy plant growth. The strip-till toolbar is useful for cultivating the soil for wide-row crops, such as corn, sugar beets, or sunflowers.

HISTORY

Illinois farmer Rich Follmer invented the strip-till toolbar in 1988. Follmer wanted a way to till the land he needed for planting while leaving the rest of the soil undisturbed. He built a homemade toolbar with 12 rows for planting seeds. Soon Follmer was producing and selling his strip-till toolbar.

SUBSOILERS

Farmers use subsoilers to break up hard soil. A subsoiler is usually pulled by a tractor. It can break up hard soil at greater depths than a plow or tiller. Compacted layers of soil can typically be found about 12 to 22 inches (30 to 56 cm) below the surface. When plant roots reach this compacted layer of soil, they stop growing. Subsoilers can break up the packed soil up to 24 inches (61 cm) below the surface.

The claws on a subsoiler are called shanks.

When soil is densely packed, water does not seep into the ground easily. The subsoiler helps loosen the soil so that crops can get the water they need.

HISTORY

Agricultural engineer Gordon Tupper invented the subsoiler in 1972. His research focused on cotton harvesting. As Tupper's subsoiler was tested, it showed a significant increase in cotton yields. His simple U-shaped machine was called the Stoneville Parabolic Subsoiler.

Subsoilers look like giant claws built to cut deep into the soil. Where the subsoiler breaks up the ground, roots can grow deeper. Water can penetrate the soil to reach those roots.

SWATHERS

A swather can be pulled by a tractor or be self-propelled. The swather uses discs or a bar to cut through the stems of hay or grain crops. After cutting, the swather neatly drops the cut stalks on the ground in windrows.

The swather is also called a windrower.

HOW THEY WORK

Historians consider Cyrus McCormick's 1830s reaper the first swather. Swathers are most popular with farmers in the northern United States and Canada, where growing seasons are shorter. Crops need to dry quickly.

The swather lays the stalks all in the same direction. This helps air and sunlight reach even the lower layers. The sun can then more easily dry the crop before it is harvested. In the southern United States where the growing seasons are longer, crops can be left standing in the fields longer. The crops dry while they are standing. Then farmers in those areas harvest them using a combine.

Flax is one crop that swathers lay in windrows. People then collect fibers from the flax stems to make linen fabric.

Tree shakers are used to harvest almonds. The almonds are left on the ground for a few days to dry.

TREE SHAKERS

A tree shaker is used to harvest fruits and nuts from trees. The tree shaker is a tractor-like vehicle with a large mechanical arm that shakes a tree trunk until the nuts or fruit drop to the ground. Tree shakers harvest fruits such as cherries, plums, apples, and olives. They also harvest nuts such as pecans, almonds, pistachios, and walnuts. Farmers usually have a tarp or net under the tree to catch the falling fruits or nuts.

TASKS

The arm that clamps on the tree has to grab the tree with just the right amount of pressure. If it is too tight, the tree trunk can be damaged. The shaker needs to shake the tree just enough to make the mature fruits or nuts fall to the ground. Some fruits, such as apples, bruise easily if dropped. So companies are working to develop vacuum harvesters. These harvesters have robotic arms that take hold of the apples using suction instead of dropping them to the ground.

Workers lay tarps to catch olives shaken from trees.

GLOSSARY

autonomous
Operating on its own without human involvement.

cultivate
To loosen or break up the soil and remove weeds in order to raise crops.

diesel
A type of fuel made from crude oil or plant matter that produces more energy than the same amount of gasoline.

feces
Solid waste from an animal; poop.

fiber
A material that can be spun into yarn.

Global Positioning System (GPS)
A satellite network that helps people determine precise locations on Earth.

harvest
The season's gathering of crops; also, to gather crops.

herbicide
A substance used to kill unwanted plants such as weeds.

hydraulics
The use of pressurized liquids to power a machine.

insecticide
A chemical used to kill insects that destroy plants.

patent
To get an official document that prevents other people from making and selling an invention.

prototype
An early model of a product or machine.

rotor
A part in a machine that rotates and sometimes has blades.

thresh
To separate grain or seeds from the rest of the plant.

windrow
Cut stalks heaped up in long rows to dry.

TO LEARN MORE

FURTHER READINGS

Lim, Angela. *The Crop Encyclopedia*. Abdo, 2025.

Macmillan, Don. *The Complete Book of Classic John Deere Tractors: The First 100 Years*. Motorbooks, 2020.

Pripps, Robert N., and Andrew Morland. *The Complete Book of Classic Ford Tractors: Every Model 1917–1996*. Motorbooks, 2021.

ONLINE RESOURCES

To learn more about tractors and equipment, please visit **abdobooklinks.com** or scan this QR code. These links are routinely monitored and updated to provide the most current information available.

INDEX

PHOTO CREDITS

Cover Photos: James Hime/Shutterstock Images, front (SAME tractor); Shutterstock Images, front (drone, McCormick tractor, John Deere tractor, hay bale), back (green mower); Rodney Hutchinson/Shutterstock Images, front (Ford tractor); Gestalt Imagery/Shutterstock Images, front (Oliver tractor), back (orange tractor); BG Media/Shutterstock Images, front (CLAAS tractor); Pavlo Baliukh/Shutterstock Images, front (New Holland tractor)
Interior Photos: Shutterstock Images, 1, 7, 8, 26, 30–31, 33, 35, 36–37, 41, 43, 44–45, 79, 84–85, 94–95, 97, 115, 118–119 (bottom), 120, 122, 123, 125, 126, 130, 131, 132, 134, 138–139, 141, 142, 143, 144, 149, 150–151, 156, 159, 166, 167, 174, 175, 183; Valentin Valkov/Shutterstock Images, 2–3, 11; CRS Photo/Shutterstock Images, 4; SSPL/Getty Images, 5; Library of Congress, 6, 16, 20, 67, 71; Universal History Archive/Universal Images Group/Getty Images, 9, 24–25, 68; Jarek Pawlak/Shutterstock Images, 10; Karen Foley Photography/Shutterstock Images, 12–13; Volodimir Bazyuk/Shutterstock Images, 13; Cara Taylor/The Washington Post/Getty Images, 14; Hulton Archive/Getty Images, 15; Everett Collection/Shutterstock Images, 17; Dee Browning/Shutterstock Images, 18; iStockphoto, 18–19, 86–87, 88–89, 168; Keystone-France/Gamma-Keystone/Getty Images, 21; Karl-Josef Hildenbrand/dpa/picture alliance/Getty Images, 22; Hulton-Deutsch Collection/Corbis Historical/Getty Images, 22–23, 129; Kristof Lauwers/Shutterstock Images, 25; Anna Stills/Shutterstock Images, 27; Gerard Koudenburg/Shutterstock Images, 28; Sheryl Watson/Shutterstock Images, 29, 66; Steven Scott/Shutterstock Images, 30; Dick Kenny/Shutterstock Images, 32; Phillip Minnis/Shutterstock Images, 34; Patrick T. Fallon/AFP/Getty Images, 37; Andia/Universal Images Group/Getty Images, 38–39 (left); Uwe Anspach/dpa/picture alliance/Getty Images, 38–39 (right); Andreas Arnold/dpa/picture alliance/Getty Images, 40–41; Michel Porro/Getty Images News/Getty Images, 42–43; LightField Studios/Shutterstock Images, 45; Internet Archive, 46, 52, 74, 101; Redwood8/Dreamstime, 47; Gestalt Imagery/Shutterstock Images, 48–49, 50, 55, 56–57; VR Studio/Shutterstock Images, 51; Dave Mathias/Denver Post/Getty Images, 53; Photo 12/Universal Images Group/Getty Images, 54; Maksim Safaniuk/Shutterstock Images, 58–59; Sueddeutsche Zeitung Photo/Alamy, 59; Keith Leighton/Alamy, 60–61; Wayne Hutchinson/Farm Images/Universal Images Group/Getty Images, 62–63; Claudia Harms-Warlies/Shutterstock Images, 63; Mark Boulton/Alamy, 64; Bernd Wittelsbach/Mauritius Images GmbH/Alamy, 65; Peter Jordan/Alamy, 69; Bettmann/Getty Images, 70; Hulton Archive/Archive Photos/Getty Images, 72; Bluetoes67/Dreamstime, 73; Rmhermen/Wikimedia Commons, 75; Wikimedia Commons, 76–77, 91, 108–109; Smith Collection/Gado/Archive Photos/Getty Images, 78; Miro Vrlik Photography/Shutterstock Images, 80; James MacDonald/Bloomberg/Getty Images, 80–81; Alex Cimbal/Shutterstock Images, 82–83; Jeffrey Greenberg/Universal Images Group/Getty Images, 85; *Gazetteer of the Manufactures and Manufacturing Towns of the United States*/J. M. Bradstreet & Son/1866/Google Books, 90; Andrew Harker/Shutterstock Images, 92–93; Image Property of New Holland Agriculture, 96, 100; Daniel Acker/Bloomberg/Getty Images, 98, 99; A. R. Coster/Topical Press Agency/Hulton Archive/Getty Images, 102; Museum of Science and Industry, Chicago/Archive Photos/Getty Images, 103; Sergei Nezhinskii/Dreamstime, 104–105; James Hime/Shutterstock Images, 106; Lukasz Szwaj/Shutterstock Images, 107; Iryna Denysova/Shutterstock Images, 108; Prashanth Vishwanathan/Bloomberg/Getty Images, 110, 111; Rahmad Himawan/Shutterstock Images, 112–113; Melnikov Dmitriy/Shutterstock Images, 114–115; Sebastian Willnow/dpa-Zentralbild/picture alliance/Getty Images, 116; Tim Leedy/MediaNews Group/Reading Eagle/Getty Images, 117; David Cole/Alamy, 118–119 (top); Jim Lambert/Shutterstock Images, 121; Rabyrd/Dreamstime, 124–125; Nicholas Smith/iStockphoto, 127; Corbis Historical/Getty Images, 128–129; Sandra J. Milburn/The Hutchinson News/AP Images, 133; Mark Brandon/Shutterstock Images, 134–135; Chris Allan/Shutterstock Images, 136; Lasse Johansson/Shutterstock Images, 137; Patnaree Asavacharanitich/Shutterstock Images, 138; Stephen William Robinson/Shutterstock Images, 140; WilleeCole Photography/Shutterstock Images, 145; Mariia Boiko/Shutterstock Images, 146–147; Elena Photos/Shutterstock Images, 147; David Calvert/Shutterstock Images, 148; Bronwyn Photo/Shutterstock Images, 150; Bayu Widhi Nugroho/Shutterstock Images, 152–153; Ionov Artem/Shutterstock Images, 153; Derek Tilley/USDA/NRCS, 154; Bob Pool/Shutterstock Images, 154–155; Andrew Aitchison/In Pictures/Getty Images, 156–157; Luce Morin/Shutterstock Images, 158; Joseph Kreiss/Shutterstock Images, 160; Igor Klyakhin/Shutterstock Images, 161; Deyana Stefanova Robova/Shutterstock Images, 162–163; Janusz Stepien/Shutterstock Images, 163; Paul Burr/Shutterstock Images, 164–165; Petr Salinger/Shutterstock Images, 165; Gary C. Tognoni/Shutterstock Images, 169; Peter Titmuss/Shutterstock Images, 170; Alexandru Logel/Shutterstock Images, 171; Jan Toula/Shutterstock Images, 172; Tonko Oosterink/Shutterstock Images, 173; Olivier Guiberteau/Shutterstock Images, 176–177; Vladimir Nenezic/Shutterstock Images, 177; Sebastien Salom-Gomis/AFP/Getty Images, 178; Matthias Mumme/Dreamstime, 179; Maksim Pipchanka/Shutterstock Images, 180; Shultay Baltaay/Shutterstock Images, 181; SKT Studio/Shutterstock Images, 182; Dmitry Strong/Shutterstock Images, 184–185; Dmitriy Kazitsyn/Shutterstock Images, 185; Michaela Warthen/Shutterstock Images, 186; Anna Fedorova/Shutterstock Images, 187

ABDOBOOKS.COM
Published by Abdo Reference, a division of ABDO, PO Box 398166, Minneapolis, Minnesota 55439.

Printed in China.
052024
092024

Editor: Marie Pearson
Series Designer: Colleen McLaren
Production Designer: Karli Kruse, Laura Kuchar

LIBRARY OF CONGRESS CONTROL NUMBER: 2023949523

PUBLISHER'S CATALOGING-IN-PUBLICATION DATA

Names: McKinney, Donna B., author.
Title: The tractor and equipment encyclopedia / by Donna B. McKinney
Description: Minneapolis, Minnesota: Abdo Reference, 2025 | Series: Farming encyclopedias | Includes online resources and index.
Identifiers: ISBN 9781098294342 (lib. bdg.) | ISBN 9798384913610 (ebook)
Subjects: LCSH: Farm tractors--Juvenile literature. | Farm equipment--Juvenile literature. | Agriculture--Equipment and supplies--Juvenile literature. | Agriculture--Juvenile literature. | Farming--Juvenile literature. | Encyclopedias and dictionaries--Juvenile literature.
Classification: DDC 629.2252--dc23